Childhood Speech, Language, and Listening Problems

What Every Parent Should Know

Patricia McAleer Hamaguchi

John Wiley & Sons, Inc.

New York • Chichester • Brisbane • Toronto • Singapore

Library of Congress Cataloging-in-Publication Data:

Hamaguchi, Patricia McAleer.
    Childhood speech, language, and listening problems : what
every parent should know / Patricia McAleer Hamaguchi.
        p.   cm.
    Includes bibliographical references and index.
    ISBN 0-471-03413-4 (paper)
    1. Communicative disorders in children—Popular works.   I. Title.
RJ496.C67H35   1995
618.92′855—dc20   94-27556

Printed in the United States of America

10 9 8 7 6 5 4 3 2 1

To my husband, Norihito,
for his unwavering support and
patience throughout this project.

And to my father, Frank McAleer, who taught me
the power of words and
my mother, Joan McAleer, who taught me
the value of listening.

Acknowledgments

I would like to thank the following people for their help throughout this project: My husband, Norihito, who endured (without complaint) hurried dinners as I wrote late into the night. Alison Picard, my agent, for her encouragement and professionalism. Judith N. McCarthy, my editor at John Wiley, for her sensitivity to this subject and dedication to turning out a quality book. My sister, Jennifer Mayo, whose need for information about children's speech and language problems provided further inspiration for me to write this. My sister, Susan Atkinson, a fellow speech pathologist, who helped me fine-tune some of the language and issues in the book. My family and friends who didn't see me or talk to me for weeks or months at a time as I worked on this and were still speaking to me when I finished: Mom, Dad, Jen, Sue, Keith, Frank, Heather, Janet, Gina H., Gina M., Janine, Viki, Pam, and Mary. Judy Albert, my colleague, who provided valuable perspective as a parent and speech pathologist. My boss, Dr. Norman Bond, who helped me become computer-literate and supported me throughout this project. My principal, Cheryl Dwyer, who understood why I needed to leave on time so many days when I would rather have served on another committee (just kidding, Cheryl). Ken Albanese, editor of the "Communication Exchange," who let me pick his brain about speech therapy services in Canada. Gail Houle and Rod Pelton from the Department of Education in Washington, D.C., who graciously spent their time answering my litany of questions. Bonnie Pike, Bernice Albert, and Susan Karr from the American Speech-Language-Hearing Association (ASHA), who looked up facts and sent me lots of good information. The National Information Center for Children and Youth with Handicaps (NICHCY), who responded so kindly to my requests for information. Kelly Hicks from the Canadian Association of Speech-Language Pathologists and Audiologists, who took the time to speak with me. Dr. Keat-Jin Lee for reviewing the book from a medical point of view. Dr. Sandra Holley for her support, despite a very busy schedule. Kathy Kelly and Jan Frietag for reviewing the book from a parent's point of view. And last, and perhaps most important, the many parents I have worked with who have entrusted me with the responsibility of helping their children learn to speak and listen better. I consider myself blessed to have had the opportunity to know you and your children. I hope I have answered all your questions in this book.

Contents

Contents

Introduction

Sometimes when I try to think of what I want to say, uh . . . the words get um . . . jumbled up in my head. . . . When the teacher calls on me in class, I can't think of it fast enough, so uh . . . I just say "I don't know." I wish I wasn't so stupid.
—Jared, age 9

Sometimes I don't understand what Miss Rodriguez is talking about. I've heard the words before, but I forget what they mean. When I have to write my spelling words in sentences, I hate it! I kinda know what they mean, but not exactly. When I read stories, I don't understand what's going on. And when I take tests in class, I forget everything. All the names and places start to sound the same. Maybe my teacher is right; if I really tried, I could do better.
—Janet, age 10

Little Red Riding Hood is about a wolf and-and-and-he putted on Grandma's clothes and she's pickin' flowers and she doesn't know it's him so he's-uh-she's in the closet and boy is she scared! She thinks it's her, but she gots tricked, so the wolf chases her . . . is that your game on the shelf?
—Michelle, age 7

1

*Yesterday Mrs. Sauer was telling us what to do, and I couldn't re-
member what she said, so I asked Jamaal 'cause he's smart. When
she caught me askin' him, she got really mad because she said I
should pay attention better, but the words just fly out of my head like
a bird.*

—Tamina, age 5

*Jessica is a very bright child, so I know there can't be anything wrong
with her. Besides, we've given her so much stimulation from the time
she was in the womb! Still, my sister keeps telling me that maybe she
should be saying more than a few words at 2½ years old. My pediatrician doesn't seem concerned, so I guess I'll just wait a few
years and see if she outgrows it.*

—Mother of Jessica, age 2½

*I know Tatiana is a bright girl. She gets straight As in math and is a
whiz in art, music, and PE! I think that's because she likes those
classes better. She just sits and stares at the paper for half the period
during language arts. If I prod her, she'll put a few words down every
once in a while, but it's like pulling teeth. If she had a learning disability, she wouldn't be such a good reader, right? So she must just
be lazy, I guess.*

—F. G., teacher

*Most of the time I can figure out what Ben wants from us. We've
developed a "code" if you will. For example, I know when he says
"gogga" he wants me to take him in the car somewhere. I feel bad
when other people don't understand him, but we've learned to be
good translators. It's not a problem for us, so why bother subjecting
him to speech therapy? I wouldn't want him to feel like he's different
from the other kids. Besides, I heard that most kids outgrow this stuff.
If he doesn't, they can work with him when he gets to kindergarten.*

—Father of Ben, age 4

These are the voices of children with communication disorders—and the
adults in their lives. If these voices sound familiar, then you have found
the right book. I wrote it for parents like you. Perhaps you suspect, but
aren't sure, whether your son or daughter has a speech, language, or

listening problem. Or maybe you are already sure but would like to have more understanding and information. Armed with knowledge, you are in a better position to help make your child's life more fulfilling and far less anguished. Despite all the other caregivers, teachers, and specialists who touch a child's life, parents need to be the most educated about their children and what they need. You are your child's best advocate!

This book is about the most common speech, language, and listening problems of children; it does not, however, address the cases in which there are psychological or psychiatric reasons for these problems. If your child's problems are rooted in those areas, you will find many books available from experts in child psychology and psychiatry that will better serve your needs. Also, although *language* can include the literary skills of reading, writing, and spelling, this book focuses only on language that is heard or spoken. Because reading and writing involve other areas (such as visual-perceptual skills or motor coordination), they are best discussed by professionals who are experts in those areas.

If you suspect or have been told that your child has a speech, language, or listening problem, you are far from alone. The most recent estimates indicate that nearly a million children between the ages of 6 and 21 receive speech and language special education services in the U.S. public schools. Another 367,083 children between the ages of 3 and 5 receive some sort of preschool special education assistance (according to the *14th Annual Report to Congress Regarding Implementation of IDEA Legislation*, 1990–91 school year). These figures tell us that nearly one-quarter of all children who receive *any* kind of special education services do, in fact, receive speech and language therapy services as well. In addition to these children, there are undoubtedly more who could benefit from receiving therapy services or consultation if they were diagnosed properly.

A Note on Definitions

The basic formula underpinning this book is $C = S + L + L$, or Communication equals **S**peech plus **L**anguage plus **L**istening. "Speech" is the process of producing meaningful sounds or words; "language" is the content of speech, the meaning of words; "listening" is the process of receiving and understanding those words. I've tried to use terminology that is familiar to most people and, at the same time, consistent with professional usage. You'll discover as you read the book that this balancing act is not always easy. For example, what I call "listening disorders" are sometimes referred to as "auditory disorders" or "receptive language deficits." You'll have to put up with a bit of jargon here and there, but I'll try to translate as we go along. In any case, learning the vocabulary will help you better understand your child's communication problems.

How to Use This Book

Part One contains general information that any parent who has, or might have, a child with a communication problem needs to know. Chapter 1 introduces you to the field and expands on the definitions of speech, language, and listening. It explains how children learn to communicate—defining the parent's role in that process—and identifies the skills and behaviors common to children of various ages. Chapter 2 tells you when to get help from trained professionals and details the warning signs of potential problems for your child. Chapter 3 helps you decide which professional to see and describes what services are available at the different institutions (school, hospitals, private clinics, and so on). It also walks you through the often confusing evaluation process. An explanation of the data and jargon in the evaluation report is provided in chapter 4. This chapter also describes what happens after the evaluation, that is, what your responsibilities and options for therapy are. You'll probably want to read all of Part One carefully.

Part Two examines particular communication problems in much more detail. You may be more selective in your perusal of these chapters, but please understand that many of the conditions they describe are interrelated (C = S + L + L). Chapters 5, 6, and 7 cover speech, language, and listening problems, respectively. I explain the diagnosis, characteristics, and treatment. I describe how your child might be affected socially and at home and school, and I explain how you can help your child cope and improve. Chapter 8 discusses causes or related conditions associated with speech, language, and listening problems such as lead poisoning, frequent ear infections, head trauma, cleft palate, Down syndrome, autism, cerebral palsy, and others.

Key terms that are defined in the glossary are set in bold when they first appear in the text.

Children with speech, language, or listening problems can look forward to less frustration, self-doubt, and misplaced blame for their limitations if they are properly diagnosed and treated and if their family is informed and supportive. No child should dread going to school or having a simple conversation! There is much that you can do to help your child be well adjusted and reach his or her fullest potential.

PART I

What You Should Know and How to Get Help

1

Speech, Language, and Listening: How They Develop

When you said "Good morning" today, and someone answered in kind, the exchange didn't strike you as particularly complicated. In fact, you were using your highly developed powers of speech, language, and listening—all part of your hard-won ability to communicate. As a parent, it is important to remember that communication is not always as easy for your child as it is now for you as an adult. After reading this chapter, you'll have a deeper appreciation of just how complex a child's path to effective communication really is.

Children start on the road to successful communication as soon as they are born. However, they progress at different rates. Some advance seemingly overnight from speaking single words to forming complete sentences that make sense. Other children take a slow, steady course with small steps, gradually adding words and building up to sentences. Often, both types of travelers reach their destination—learning to communicate equally well—in their own time, without any special attention. Members of a third group, however, need a little extra help along the way.

How is your child's communication journey going? Is he or she traveling more or less in step with one of the first two groups; that is (the dreaded question), is he or she "progressing normally"?

When discussing childhood development, the word *normal* projects a powerful aura of good and right, perhaps because *abnormal* is not a label we want attached to our children. Please understand, however, that normal, as used by educators and therapists, is a nonthreatening statistical term, better defined as *typical* or *average*. Developmental standards for what the professionals call normal have been established after years of observation and study of children who are considered to be free of such handicapping conditions as deafness or cerebral palsy. Indeed, within the parameters of normal, you will find a wide range of standards.

How can two children who exhibit different language abilities *both* be considered normal? Because, even within each age group, each child has an individual developmental timetable. For example, Roberto may acquire the language behaviors of the 2-to-3 age group just before his second birthday, whereas Mark may be just beginning to display those behaviors as he approaches his third birthday. Both of these boys fall into the normal category. Just because two children of the same age have markedly different communication patterns does not mean that one of them has a problem, particularly in the younger age groups.

Later in this chapter, I'll explain how children learn to communicate. Then I detail the important communication milestones for the many age groupings, ranging from birth to adolescence. First, however, we need to share a common vocabulary. Just as we "pros" have our own sense of normal, so too, do we have our own definition of *communication*. Actually, our communication is much like the everyday variety. It is best understood through the three central skill components: speech, language, and listening. Knowing what's involved in these three areas is the first step in understanding what difficulties your child may be having and thus is the beginning of being able to help.

What Is Speech?

Speech refers to the sounds that come out of our mouths and take shape in the form of words. You realize just how complex the speech process really is when you study it or if you lose the ability to produce speech effortlessly.

Many things must happen in order for us to speak:

- The brain must create an idea it wants to communicate to someone else.
- The brain must then send that idea to the mouth.
- The brain must tell the mouth which words to say and which sounds make up those words. Intonation patterns and accented syllables must be incorporated.

- The brain must also send the proper signals to the muscles that produce speech: those that control the tongue, the lips, and the jaw.
- These muscles must have the strength and coordination to carry out the brain's commands.
- The lungs must have sufficient air and the muscles in the chest must be strong enough to force the vocal cords to vibrate. The air must be going out, not in, for functional speech to occur.
- The vocal cords must be in good working condition for speech to sound clear and be loud enough to be heard.
- The words produced must be monitored by our hearing sense. This helps us review what is said and hear new words to imitate in other situations. If words are not heard clearly, speech will be equally "mumbly" when reproduced.
- Another person must be willing to communicate with us and listen to what we say. If no one is listening and reacting to our speech, there is no point in speaking.

For most children, these processes happen naturally, if proper stimulation occurs, without conscious thought. For some children, this sequence breaks down. Once the source of the breakdown is identified, these steps can be facilitated in a direct and conscious manner.

What Is Language?

Language refers to the content of what is spoken, written, read, or understood. Language can also be gestural, as when we use body language or sign language. It is categorized into two areas: receptive and expressive. The ability to comprehend someone else's speech or gestures is called **receptive language.** The ability to create a spoken message that others will understand is called **expressive language.**

In order for children to understand and use spoken language in a meaningful way, these things must happen:

- Their ears must hear well enough for the child to distinguish one word from another.
- Someone must show, or model, what words mean and how sentences are put together.
- The ears must hear intonation patterns, accents, and sentence patterns.

- The brain must have enough intellectual capability to process what those words and sentences mean.
- The brain must be able to store all this information so it can be retrieved later.
- The brain must have a way to recreate words and sentences heard previously when it wants to communicate an idea to someone else.
- Children must have the physical ability to speak in order for the words to be heard and understood when used.
- Children must have a psychological or social need and interest to use these words and communicate with others.
- Another interested person must reinforce attempts at communication.

Children with receptive language problems can be described as having **listening disorders** as well, since listening is the most common way we receive language information. It is our brain's input. A child with a receptive language problem may find activities such as listening to classroom lectures, comprehending stories heard or read, following conversations, or remembering oral directions confusing and frustrating at times.

If a child's receptive language is not developed, the entire language learning process stalls before it even begins. Parents tend to be more concerned if their child isn't talking the way they expect, but speech-language pathologists also want to find out if the child is hearing clearly and understanding language. If not, meaningful speech (expressive language) is not going to develop. That is why "speech" therapy often focuses on strengthening receptive language skills, even if the concern is that the child isn't talking properly.

Speech is the physical process of forming the words; expressive language is what that speech creates—the output, or the product. Even if we have the capability to produce understandable speech sounds, we cannot communicate if what we say is meaningless or confusing to others. We must use words that others can comprehend and put them together in sentences that have order and flow. These words and sentences can be spoken, written, or gestured. Children with expressive language problems may use words incorrectly (e.g., "He falled down"); they may have difficulty organizing and sequencing their thoughts, as well as learning the names of things; and they may dislike engaging in lengthy conversations. It is also not uncommon for children with expressive language problems to have difficulty pronouncing words.

Many children with language problems have difficulty with both receptive and expressive language. They may also possess weak listening skills, since strong listening abilities are needed to receive and develop language.

What Is Listening?

Listening is an active process of hearing and comprehending what is said. As with speech, several steps must occur for us to listen:

- Sound waves must carry the spoken words to our ears.
- The sound must travel through the outer ear canals without obstruction.
- The sound must then pass through the eardrum and middle ear without being distorted by fluid from colds, infection, or allergies.
- It then travels through the inner ear, which must be functioning properly as well.
- This sound travels via the auditory nerve to the brain.
- The brain tries to compare what it hears to previously stored sounds and words to make sense of the message.

Good listening is as critical a part of the communication process as clear speaking and choosing the right words, because communication is a two-way process. One person sends a message, and, ideally, someone else will receive it the way it was intended. Who likes to talk to someone who doesn't pay attention to what is said? Who enjoys repeating things over and over without the desired response? Who wants to be misunderstood? No one, of course. A child with a listening disorder will certainly test your patience, but she is probably even more frustrated than you are.

Your child's frustration may translate into behaviors that can be misunderstood as ignoring you, not paying attention, or stupidity. A child with listening problems will have difficulty coping in a classroom situation, because so much of the information teachers give to students must be heard. With the right help, however, a child can learn to cope and to improve listening skills.

If the brain can't stay focused on the task of listening long enough to translate the information, the message will be lost. This is what happens with an **auditory memory** problem. With an **attention deficit** problem, the brain works on too many projects at once and can't stay with a message long enough to finish comprehending it. If the brain has difficulty storing old information, it will not know how to integrate the new information or make sense of it. An **auditory comprehension** or **auditory processing** problem may result. These are examples of just a few listening disorders.

How Do Children Learn to Communicate?

You may think communication begins with a child's first words, but a great deal of preparation must take place before that first word is uttered.

Communication Begins with You

Babies need someone to interact with them and encourage them in a loving way. Placing a baby in front of a television exposes a child to some language, but it's a passive process. A baby needs to be actively engaged with people in order for the communication experience to be meaningful. I can't overstate the importance of a parent's interest and interaction with a child, from infancy on, in developing a child's communication skills.

The receptors in a child's brain need to be stimulated, particularly during the early learning years. These receptors are stimulated when the child is touched, spoken to, and shown pictures, objects, places, and people. Without proper nurturing, a child may experience learning delays, or speech, language, or listening disorders.

In many cases, a parent's stimulation can make the difference between a child with below-average or above-average communication abilities. Information must have a way of getting into the brain. If no one helps to put information in, the brain will not be adept at processing it once information is received in school. Unfortunately, many children do experience communication problems, regardless of the amount or quality of early stimulation.

The Communication-Learning Process

Babies practice using their brains to produce the sounds that come out of their mouths. For infants, the sound comes out as crying. As infants' lungs and mouths develop strength and control, they can make the cries sound the way they want. They learn to intensify their cries when they are really upset and to temper them when they are just uncomfortable or hungry.

Around 3 to 6 months of age, babies experiment with their mouths and find they can make some babbling sounds, which often get a lot of attention from the people around them. If they get noticed, they will do it more. They have even more fun when people repeat the sounds back to them. Babies listen to the words people say and try to figure out what they mean.

Other developmental milestones such as eating solids, developing certain play behaviors, and maintaining good physical health may play a role in the communication-learning process as well. You should familiarize yourself with these other developmental milestones. There are entire books written, for example, by Dr. Spock and T. Berry Brazelton, that detail them for you.

Sometimes a problem in one of these areas can affect a child's rate of speech and language development. For example, if a child who has had frequent ear infections coupled with a delay in speaking is brought to me, I might suspect some residual fluid lingering in the middle ear. This problem needs to be medically resolved in order for meaningful speech to occur. I would urge the parents to take their child to an audiologist and an ear, nose, and throat doctor. If eating and walking were difficult for the child in addition to pronouncing words, a motor problem (difficulty moving muscles normally) might be the underlying culprit. In this case, I would refer the family to a physical or occupational therapist, or even a neurologist.

Your daughter or son must always be seen in terms of the "whole child." By focusing exclusively on individual parts of the child, we cannot know if all the other parts are doing exactly what they should. That is why team evaluations are such a good idea, particularly for infants and preschool children.

Speech, Language, and Listening Milestones

Your child will probably begin to exhibit the following behaviors at the ages shown in the following lists. Use these as a general guide. As stated before, every child is unique. If your child exhibits most of the behaviors for his age, there is no need for concern. If some skills have not yet developed, read chapter 2 to see if you need to consult a specialist at this point in time.

Birth to 3 Months
- Reacts to sudden noises by crying or jerking body
- Reacts to familiar objects, such as a bottle, or familiar people, such as parents

- Differentiates the cry of pain from the cry of hunger
- Coos, begins to form prolonged vowels with changes in intonation ("Ahhhh-AH-ahhh!")
- Watches objects intently

3 to 6 Months

- Begins to babble, using syllables with a consonant and vowel ("baa-ba-BA-ba-ba!") and uses intonation changes
- Laughs and shows pleasure when happy
- Turns the head to see where sound is coming from
- Reacts when his or her name is heard
- Uses a louder voice for crying and babbling than before
- Shows delight when bottle or breast is presented

6 to 9 Months

- Begins to comprehend simple words such as *no* and looks at family members when they are named
- Babbles with a singsong pattern at times
- Controls babbling to two syllables, which sometimes sounds like words such as *Mama*, although meaning is, typically, not understood by the baby yet
- Understands facial expressions and reacts to them
- Attempts gestures to correspond to pat-a-cake and bye-bye
- Shakes head to show *no*
- Uses more and more sounds when babbling, such as syllables with *da, ba, ka, pa, ma,* and *wa*

9 to 12 Months

- Has fun imitating simple sounds and babbling
- Begins to say "Mama" or "Dada" with meaning
- Begins to understand that words represent objects
- Jabbers loudly
- Responds to music
- Gives or seeks a toy or common object when requested
- Imitates common animal sounds
- Gestures and whines to request something
- Looks directly at the source of sound immediately

12 to 18 Months

- Understands 50 to 75 words
- Uses 3 to 20 "real" words, even if not produced completely clearly

- Points to known objects when named
- Points to a few simple body parts, such as eyes and nose
- Babbles and uses nonsense words while pointing
- Follows simple one-step commands
- Uses words like *more, all-gone, mine,* and *down*
- Imitates words
- Pronounces some understandable words
- Typical utterances at this age:
  "Mama!"
  "No!"
  "Daddy, doppit!" (stop it)
  "Appuh" (apple)
  "Gimme da!" (give me that)
  "Baw" (ball)
  "Too-duh" (toothbrush)

18 Months to 2 Years
- Comprehends about 300 words
- Uses about 50 recognizable words, mostly nouns
- Speaks with mostly "real" words now
- Wants to hear the same stories over and over
- Uses rising intonation pattern to show a question
- Shakes head to answer yes/no questions ("Do you want more milk?")
- Follows two related commands ("Go upstairs and get your bottle.")
- Begins to use some verbs (*go*) and adjectives (*big*)
- Joins two related words to make one word (*geddown* for *get down* or *stoppit* for *stop it*)
- Starts to ask, "What's 'at?" (what's that)
- Talks about what is happening now
- Tells you his or her name when asked
- Joins in nursery rhymes and songs
- Speaks with many pauses between words
- Typical utterances at this age:
  "Dawddie bad!" (Doggie bad!)
  "Go 'way!" (Go away!)
  "No, Mommy."
  "See . . . horsey, . . . Daddy!"
  "Danwit . . . goo'. . . Mommy." (Sandwich good, Mommy.)
  "Nigh'-nigh' now?" (Night-night now?)
  "Go dore?" (Go store?)

2 to 3 Years
- Understands about 900 words
- Uses about 500 words
- Pronounces words more clearly
- Engages in eye contact during conversations with occasional prompting
- Makes frustrations known more with words and less with temper tantrums and crying
- Sits and listens to stories for 10 to 20 minutes
- Identifies a *boy* and *girl*
- Answers simple questions beginning with *who, where,* and *what* ("Who drives a firetruck?")
- Understands prepositions such as *in, on,* and so forth
- Begins to ask yes/no questions ("It raining?")
- Talks to self while playing
- Begins to use function words such as *is* ("Ball is red")
- Begins to use past tense verbs (*walked, kicked*)
- "Stutters" when excited sometimes
- Pronounces these sounds consistently in words: *m, n, p, f, b, d, h, y, m*
- Typical utterances at this age:
  "Daddy's tar . . . so big!" (Daddy's car so big)
  "Mommy put dat downdairs?" (Mommy put that downstairs?)
  "Oh no! My-my-my jeth iddirty!" (Oh no! My dress is dirty.)
  "You wanna 'nana, An' Pat?" (You want a banana, Aunt Pat?)
  "I doe wannit!" (I don't want it)
  "Mattchew's yeg beedin'!" (Matthew's leg bleeding)
  "Duh wabbit eated duh cawit!" (The rabbit eated the carrot)

3 to 4 Years
- Begins to use *is* at beginning of questions
- Understands about 1,200 words
- Uses about 800 words
- Uses eye contact more consistently during conversations
- Asks many questions, usually *what* or *who* questions
- Understands time concepts such as *morning, lunch time, tonight*
- Understands positional words such as *in front, behind, up,* and *down*
- Starts to use *s* on verbs to show present tense (he *runs*)
- Uses contractions *won't* and *can't*
- Uses *and*
- Uses plurals consistently (*books, toys*)

- Uses *are,* or contracted form, with plural nouns ("Kids're playing outside")
- Initiates conversations, making comments or observations
- Asks many questions, sometimes the same one several times in a few minutes
- Follows a simple plot in a children's storybook
- Sits down and does one activity for 10 to 15 minutes
- "Stutters" less frequently
- Pronounces the beginning, middle, and ending sounds in words, except for consonant blends (e.g., *bl, fr, cr*)
- Uses *k* and *g* sounds correctly, but *s* may still be somewhat "lispy" sounding; *r* and *l* may be distorted; *v, sh, ch, j,* and *th* still may not be used consistently
- Typical utterances at this age:
  "The bider ith cwawlin' up duh twee!" (The spider is crawling up the tree)
  "Dad, the tiddy-tat breaked the diss." (Dad, the kitty-cat breaked the dish.)
  "Is Mom-Mom comin' today?"
  "Where's the hop-sital?" (Where's the hospital?)
  "Yesterday my dog Wainbow ate six bixkits." (Yesterday my dog Rainbow ate six biscuits.)

4 to 5 Years
- Comprehends 2,500 to 2,800 words
- Uses 1,500 to 2,000 words
- Speaks clearly most of the time
- Describes pictures with complete sentences
- Makes up stories
- Uses all pronouns correctly: *he, she, I, you, them*
- Describes what you do with common objects
- Speaks in complex sentences that often run together
- Uses past, present, and future tenses of verbs (*sit, sitting, sits, sat, will sit*)
- Uses irregular verbs (*drank, ate*) and irregular nouns (*men, children*) somewhat consistently
- Follows three-step commands
- Explains events that took place in the past with accurate detail
- Knows common opposites such as *big/little, heavy/light*
- Plays dramatically and chats a lot
- Repeats a sentence with 10 to 12 syllables
- Listens and attends to stories, conversation, and movies

- Mispronounces *s, r, th, l, v, sh, ch, j* and blends
- Typical utterances at this age:

"Daddy, I wanna go to Joey's house after lunch 'cause he's got this great new truck I wanna play wif (with)."

"Is this your pocketbook? Could I thee (see) what you have inside it?"

"Do you have any gum in there?"

"I found all these wed (red) marbles on José's floor, Mommy. Can I have them? I want to play with them for a little while."

"Look at all those gwirrels (squirrels) runnin' across the road!"

"Johnnie cutted the paper all up."

5 to 7 Years: The Refinement Years

- Refines pronunciation, sentence structure, word use, attention span for listening, and memory for directions
- Increases vocabulary; incorporates new words into spontaneous speech
- Retells stories; explains experiences more, in a cohesive, sequential manner and with greater elaboration
- Participates in group discussions and takes turns in conversation; comments are more relative to topic being discussed
- Begins to learn language relationships: opposites (*big/little, sad/happy*), synonyms (*big/large, sad/unhappy*), (associations *bread/butter, pencil/eraser*), and classification (*shirt/pants/socks* belong in the category of *clothing*)
- Typical utterances at this age:

"Last week Daddy took me and Levonne to the Bronx Zoo."

"You shoulda seen the monkeys and elephants!"

"On the way home, we stopped at the hospital to see Mrs. Stro . . . strogin . . . hausen . . . something like that—she's Daddy's friend from work."

"She has 'amonia and she's really sick, so she has to stay in the hopsital for another week."

When children begin school, language is translated into written symbols through spelling and comprehended through reading. Written words are developed into sentences and stories. Children whose oral language is deficient (beyond the typical errors a child of this age displays) are at risk for reading, writing, and spelling problems. However, teachers are trained to teach children in a way that best suits their individual needs. So, although communication problems may present a challenge, they certainly can be managed with a little bit of teamwork, creativity, and patience!

7 Years to Adolescence
- Possesses a functional and abstract language system
- Shows age-appropriate skills in reading, writing, speaking, and listening
- Shows less vagueness and grouping for words
- Joins sentences to form coherent, descriptive thoughts and stories; listeners are not left confused
- Masters word relationships (synonyms, antonyms, association, classification, etc.)
- Pronounces multisyllabic words correctly once practiced a few times
- Comprehends information heard and read when adequately taught and explained
- Understands and uses more idoms (*pain in the neck, out of your mind*)
- Understands plots with increasing depth and complexity when read or watched in a movie or television show
- Typical utterances at this age:
  Essentially, a child's language at this age mirrors an adult's, but with more simplicity.

These then are the milestones, the points of progress children should reach in their own style, at their own pace. The next chapter details the warning signs that signal your child may be having more than normal trouble in developing communication skills. Read on to find out how to recognize these signals and what to do to help your child deal with special problems.

2

Does Your Child Need Help? The Warning Signs

If you have any question at all regarding your child's speech, language, and listening development, it's almost always best to be on the safe side and pursue a professional opinion. This may sound simplistic, but it is important. Don't assume your child will "outgrow the problem," although many children do in time. Where do you find such a professional? Most likely at your local elementary school. All U.S. school systems must provide free screening for children if a parent is concerned, even before the child has entered school. The legal mandate comes from the Individuals with Disabilities Education Act (IDEA), Public Law 101–476. You have nothing to lose by seeking help. Neither you nor your child can afford to wait if there *is* a problem.

In this chapter, I explain why it is almost always better to seek a professional evaluation early, and I help you identify when to make that first visit. I also describe the warning signs of receptive and expressive language problems and break down by age group the signals for other speech, language, and listening problems.

When to Get Help

Children usually learn to talk in a natural way, by listening and repeating what they hear. Learning speech and language, however, does not come "naturally" for every child. Your child may need a different approach if he or she has a speech or language disorder. And earlier is *almost always* better.

There are cases where a child *is* better left alone, particularly when pronunciation problems are involved. But you should have a better idea about when to give a child some time to grow out of a speech problem after you read this book.

If you have concerns about your child's speech, language, or listening development, here are some good reasons why you should consider pursuing a professional opinion now, just to be sure:

- Research shows that a child whose language delay is identified early has a significantly better chance of developing necessary prereading and academic skills than a child whose delay is not identified early (Snyder-McLean & McLean, 1987; Stedman, 1989/90; Warren & Kaiser, 1988).
- Children who are self-conscious about their speech can develop self-esteem problems. But my experience shows that young children are less aware of their speech problems. Thus, they can be successfully remediated, in many cases, *before* they even realize their speech is different.
- From a practical point of view, it is better to assess children prior to entering school, because the testing process takes some time. That way, if your child does need help, a program will be in place upon entering kindergarten and there will be no delay in receiving assistance. Also, the classroom teacher will have better information as to which teaching strategies would be most effective for your child.
- Without professional guidance, the more you try to help your child, the more frustrating it can become. You may unintentionally hinder rather than help your child by insisting that she imitate sounds or words before being ready. A professional can tell you how to help your child without causing frustration or loss of self-esteem.
- In many cases, the speech-language pathologist may simply put your mind at ease by telling you that your child's "problem" is a very normal stage of development.

What Is the "Right Age" to Seek Help?

Unfortunately, there is no universal age at which parents should seek professional help for a speech, language, or listening problem, because every child is developmentally unique. Also, some problems are less pronounced than others and only become noticeable when a child is a little older. Hearing problems or brain injuries can occur at any age. Nevertheless, your child's communication skills can be observed by speech-language professionals and compared to children who were "developing normally" for that age. Within that relative framework, your speech-language pathologist can help you determine whether your child's communication represents a typical maturational speech or language pattern or displays warning signs that you must investigate further.

Case Study: Tawana

I saw Tawana at 2 years of age, and though she did not have advanced speech skills, she was still within that broad spectrum of what we call "average." Her language skills, however, were on the lower end of the average range, so I gave her parent some activities to do at home to give her a little boost. I asked to see Tawana again in six to eight months, just to make sure she was progressing as she should. When I saw Tawana again eight months later, she still basically spoke as she did at age 2. Of course, what is normal for a child at age 2 years, 8 months is a little more advanced than for a child who just turned 2. So Tawana's language skills were now considered below average. She had not kept up with her peers as we had hoped.

Should I have known Tawana would have problems? Should Tawana have been receiving aggressive speech therapy to prevent such problems? Did we wait too long? The answer to all these questions is no. Tawana received help at the appropriate time. Her development in other areas was age appropriate, she had no health problems, there was no family history of communication problems, and her parents were educated, nurturing people. Tawana's parents brought her in to see me as soon as they became concerned. This early intervention allowed me to keep a careful eye on her progress and to introduce help when it was appropriate and could benefit Tawana the most.

Unfortunately, predicting whether a child will have problems at a later age is usually difficult, if not impossible. We can merely examine what the child is doing *now*, stimulate growth as much as we can, and monitor progress carefully. Subjecting a child to preventive therapy in the absence of the conditions I described in the preceding case is not helpful or appropriate.

The age at which a child needs therapy depends on the child and the nature and degree of the problem. Many times a child falls into a gray area—there may be deficits in a few speech or language areas, but the child is within normal limits overall. That child may in time catch up and pass her peers, or she may fall further behind. Without a family history of problems or other variables present, there is no way to know what the future will bring.

The best thing you can do is to call a professional and explain your concerns. Chapter 3 explains how to find one.

Should You Wait until Your Child Goes to School?

When mulling over your concerns, bear in mind that a child who has a speech, language, or listening problem upon entering kindergarten will be at a distinct disadvantage for learning and participating in class.

The following are just a few of the ways speech, language, and listening skills are crucial to success in school:

- The ability to follow directions in a group setting requires an adequate attention span, knowledge of basic concepts, good hearing, and memory for spoken language.
- Learning how to sound out words and associate letters with sounds also requires good hearing, memory for sounds, and an understanding of how sounds make up words and change their meaning.
- Understanding the plot to a story requires the ability to process language and integrate previously learned words with new ones.
- Making up a story or explaining something as simple as "Show and Tell" requires the ability to put words together with organization and use a speech pattern that is understandable to others.

Getting help before kindergarten does not guarantee a trouble-free school experience. If there is a problem, however, early intervention will give your child a head start on working out a solution.

Can an Intelligent Child Have a Speech, Language, or Listening Problem?

Don't make the mistake of confusing intelligence with speech, language, or listening skills. Although children with limited intellectual abilities do have limited communication skills, children with delayed communication skills do not necessarily have below-average intelligence; they can have average to superior intelligence. These children can be gifted and talented in many, many ways. *By pursuing a speech-language evaluation, you are not questioning your child's intelligence.* A psychologist performs IQ testing, which measures a child's intellectual ability. These are two related but separate issues.

Some parents in the United States are reluctant to have their child tested out of fear of having the child "labeled" by the school system. In fact, a child who is being tested is *not* labeled as a "special education" student unless the evaluation shows a need for services and the parent consents. If your child does need help, please know *the label of "special education" has no relationship to the child's IQ.* These days, special education covers a wide range of services that children need to meet individual needs. In many cases, children with high IQ scores have special needs as well.

Warning Signs to Look For

Most parents I see are quite perceptive about their children. They often discount their observations or fears but are usually right on target. *Trust those gut feelings.* You may not know the professional lingo, but you know when something is just not "right." In addition, the following warning signs can guide you in determining whether your child may need special help for a communication problem.

Signs of a Receptive Language Problem

As we discussed in chapter 1, receptive language refers to how well a child understands and remembers what is said. The following behaviors may signal a receptive language problem:

• *Your child has difficulty understanding stories that are read aloud.* This can often be interpreted as "disinterest," but, in fact, the indifference is due to confusion or difficulty concentrating when listening.

• *Your child has difficulty with reading comprehension once she is able to read.* While remedial reading tutoring is helpful, the problem may be language-based and require additional expertise and treatment from a speech-language pathologist.

• *Your child withdraws from social conversation or tries to develop relationships through physical activities.* The athletic child who can play for hours on the playground with friends may be uncomfortable when the activities turn to conversation. As children become older, social interaction is less activity-related, and the problem may become more pronounced.

• *Your child may be very "forgetful."* Your child might appear to hear what someone is saying but really does forget what he or she is supposed to do. This behavior can often be construed as willful disobedience or "laziness." I have met very few "lazy" children. Often a legitimate reason, beyond their control, accounts for their lack of follow-through. Once you know why your child is "forgetting," you can learn how to communicate in a way your child can understand and remember.

• *Your child misconstrues what others are saying to her.* This sometimes causes hurt feelings or "acting out" behaviors. *Acting out* refers to any aggressive physical behavior, such as kicking, throwing, pushing, or hitting.

• *Your child has difficulty following directions.* Remembering what to do and doing it in the right order is hard for a child with a receptive language problem. Processing too much language at once can get confusing. Often the child may compensate by copying what other children are doing, pretending to know what to do (but often doing it incorrectly), or fooling around so he or she can avoid the task altogether.

Signs of an Expressive Language Problem

As discussed in chapter 1, expressive language refers to what the child is able to say and how it is said. The following behaviors may signal an expressive language problem:

• *Your child seldom initiates conversations and tends to give short answers to your questions.* This can sometimes be misconstrued as indicating a "shy" personality.

• *Your child overgeneralizes names of things.* For example, all drinks may be "juice" to a 4-year-old instead of labeling the drinks more specifically as "lemonade" or "iced-tea." An 11-year-old may identify a bracelet as a "thing on your hand."

• *Your child may talk in circles.* This tendency makes it difficult to make heads or tails of a story or explanation. The sequence of what happened may be backward or unclear. Very young children do this, but by age 6 or 7 this should be greatly improved.

• *Your child has difficulty remembering the names of people, places, and things.* This difficulty can be particularly noticeable in school when your child is studying for and taking tests. Filling in blanks becomes overwhelming.

• *Your child has difficulty putting sentences together with the right words or in the right order.* The words may have no endings to show plurals ("three car outside"), possessives ("Sally house is nice"), or the past tense ("He work yesterday"). Some words may be left out; for example, "Mommy dress not on a bed." This type of sentence is typical for a toddler but not for a child 4 years old or older.

Red Flag: Recurrent Ear Infections

If your child has had frequent ear infections, you should be on guard for possible delays in speech, language, and listening skills. Frequent, protracted ear infections are sometimes associated with delays in these skills years after the infections have cleared.

Red Flag: Behavior Problems

Recent research shows that many children diagnosed as "emotionally disturbed" or who display other antisocial behavior have poor language and listening skills (Mack & Warr-Leeper, 1992; Prizant et al., 1990). It is difficult to know at this point whether these communication problems *caused* the behavioral problem or whether they simply are a small piece of the puzzle for these particular children. Regardless, to help them develop their language and listening skills, they need the same understanding and treatment as is given to other children with communication problems.

Children with speech and language problems that go unaddressed sometimes cope by expressing their feelings and frustrations through their fists instead of words. Their self-esteem can suffer, which can adversely affect their whole perception of themselves, their willingness to participate in class, and their ability to have a relaxed conversation with peers. Sometimes that "class clown" is merely trying to joke his way out of not understanding the question or conversation.

Therefore, whenever a child has consistently poor social behavior, a thorough learning disabilities and speech-language evaluation should be performed as part of any testing battery. My experience is that these problems are often overlooked or referred solely to a psychologist. Although counseling and behavior modification is a very appropriate method of dealing with the behavioral symptoms, it may not be getting to the root cause of the behavior.

In my experience, many students demonstrate noticeable improvement in their behavior once their educational program is adjusted to meet their needs and they have been reassured that they are not "stupid" or "lazy." Once parents understand why their child is not following their directions or remembering conversations from breakfast, they are less apt to get angry or feel the child is deliberately ignoring them. After a language or listening problem has been properly diagnosed, a parent can learn how to communicate better with the child in a way that is less confusing and frustrating for both of them.

Other Warning Signs

Additionally, the presence of any of the following behaviors may be a warning sign of a possible speech, language, or listening problem. You should be concerned if your child:

Birth to 12 Months
- Avoids eye contact
- Rarely babbles; is unusually quiet
- Doesn't respond to whispered speech consistently
- Shows little interest in imitating gestures such as "bye-bye"
- Cries often, without changing pitch or intensity
- Shows little emotion

12 to 18 Months
- Avoids eye contact
- Doesn't say "Mama" or "Dada"
- Is unable to point to common body parts when asked
- Is unable to follow a simple one-step direction, such as "Go get the cup," unless accompanied by a gesture

18 to 24 Months
- Avoids eye contact
- Has difficulty pointing to pictures named
- Is quiet most of the time, rarely attempting to imitate or produce words
- Tunes out others frequently
- Is disinterested in talking

24 to 36 Months
- Avoids eye contact
- Has difficulty singing songs or imitating parts of simple nursery rhymes
- Has difficulty naming most common household objects
- Doesn't put short two- or three-word phrases together
- Has difficulty sitting and attending to a book or movie for more than a few minutes
- Is very difficult to understand when talking

Preschool Age (3 to 5 Years)

- Speaks differently from other children of the same age; is difficult to understand
- Has difficulty maintaining eye contact when listening or speaking
- Is disinterested or detached from other children of the same age when playing
- Makes noises or uses gestures to express needs instead of using words and sentences
- Has difficulty comprehending or following conversations (or simple oral directions)
- Watches what others are doing or needs to see gestures before attempting to follow a direction
- Speaks in short phrases instead of complete sentences most of the time
- Leaves out words such as *is* or *the* (e.g., "Patty not going in car")
- Leaves off endings (e.g., "He play with nice toy") or beginning sounds (*aw* for *straw*)

School Age (5 to 12 Years)

- Speaks differently from other children of the same age
- Experiences difficulty with reading, writing, or spelling
- Has difficulty passing tests, even after studying
- Forgets the meaning of new words
- Gropes to put words together or avoids in-depth conversations
- Has difficulty comprehending written or oral information easily
- Mispronounces multisyllabic words or new words unless repeated and practiced many times
- Sounds "babyish" or awkward at times when speaking
- Is easily distracted
- Needs verbal directions repeated
- Often says "I don't know what I'm supposed to do" after listening to directions
- Uses vague language to retell a story or event, leaving the listener confused (e.g., "That guy over there, and that big thing was next to that stuff.")
- Jumps from topic to topic or makes unrelated comments during a conversation
- Has difficulty "getting started" or answering at all when asked an open-ended question, such as "Tell me about the movie"
- Omits endings from words; leaves out or distorts sounds
- Displays behavioral or social problems
- Sounds hoarse or too deep when speaking
- Stutters

Again, if your child displays *any* of the warning signs discussed in this chapter, you should call a specialist to discuss your concerns. In the United States, talk to your pediatrician if other areas besides speech and language are delayed (particularly if your child is under the age of 2). Call a speech pathologist when your child's problem is only speech or language delays. Chapter 3 describes who to call and how to find them. At that point, the specialist can determine whether a personal meeting with your child is appropriate.

In Canada, talk to your physician if the child has not yet entered school, because speech therapy is handled as a Ministry of Health concern. Each province's protocol varies once the child reaches school. This is discussed further in chapter 3.

3

Having Your Child Evaluated

Once you've noticed some of the warning signs outlined in chapter 2, the next step is to talk to a professional. Many times a simple phone conversation is all you will need to put your mind at rest. However, in most cases the specialist needs to see your child in person to decide whether a full evaluation is warranted. But where do you start? Who do you call? And how do you know this person is qualified? This chapter discusses how to choose the right person to give your son or daughter the appropriate help. First, I define the various types of professionals available and assist you in sorting out the different titles they may go by. Next, I identify the settings in which these individuals work—private practices, public schools, hospitals, college speech clinics, agencies—listing the advantages and disadvantages of each. Finally, I describe the evaluation process itself and detail the components of the informal and formal tests your child is likely to be given.

Who to See

As discussed earlier in this book, many different professionals are available to help children experiencing communication delays. However, if your *primary* concern is your child's speech, spoken language, comprehension, or processing of spoken language, it makes the most sense to start with a **speech-language pathologist (SLP).** Once an evaluation has been completed, the speech pathologist will know whether a referral to another professional is in order. For infants and toddlers, a team evaluation may be standard procedure in your area, which allows the professionals to look at your child from different perspectives and put their collective heads together. This eliminates a lot of running around and waiting for appointments.

In Canada, speech therapy is considered the domain of the Ministry of Health. In most provinces, you should talk to your doctor first or the child's teacher if you have a concern. Some school systems in Canada have speech therapists assigned to the school or work with the Ministry of Health, which provides the therapy at a hospital. Staffing is much more limited than in the United States, and, in many cases, SLPs have long waiting lists. Often other professionals in the school, such as the classroom teacher or special education teacher, help facilitate speech and language development with the speech pathologist acting as a consultant.

In both the United States and Canada, a special education teacher (also known in some regions as a **learning disabilities consultant**) may be consulted to see whether other **learning disabilities** exist that might get in the way of reading and writing, the written forms of language. A psychologist can be helpful in assessing whether language use is being affected by emotional issues or whether the child has intellectual limitations. Usually a psychologist and/or special education teacher are the primary professionals involved with **Attention Deficit Disorder (ADD)** problems, with the speech-language pathologist contributing as a consultant or related service. This may also be true in some cases for children displaying autistic tendencies or with mental retardation.

An **audiologist** should assist in treating a child with a hearing or **central auditory processing disorder.** An **occupational therapist** is trained to facilitate development of fine motor skills, which can affect feeding as well as speaking.

Though these other specialists are important and integral parts of the team, the speech-language pathologist is uniquely qualified to properly diagnose and treat speech and oral language problems.

Speech-Language Pathologists, Speech Clinicians, Speech Therapists, and Other Labels

The terms *speech-language pathologist, speech clinician, speech pathologist,* and **speech therapist** are often used interchangeably in conversation. However, the American Speech-Language-Hearing Association (ASHA), which is the national organization that licenses speech-language pathologists in the United States, has made an effort to move away from using the terms *speech therapist* and *speech pathologist* toward using *speech-language pathologist* to better reflect the profession's orientation toward the diagnosis and treatment of language disorders. Most professionals now use speech-language pathologist on formal reports and documents. Although this is a more descriptive term, it is a bit cumbersome at times, particularly when writing a book! In the field, we sometimes shorten this designation by using the initials SLP.

In most states, speech-language pathologists are required to hold a master's degree in communication science or speech-language pathology. Licensing and certification procedures vary from state to state. School systems are required to hire only certified speech-language pathologists who also have training in school-related issues. ASHA tests and licenses on a national level and can direct you to an accredited program or nationally licensed professional. The initials **CCC-SLP** (Certificate of Clinical Competency–Speech-Language Pathology) after a speech pathologist's name indicate a national license. You can find ASHA's phone number in Appendix A.

In Canada, each province decides the educational qualifications needed to be a speech pathologist.

Where to Go

Once you have decided to consult a professional about your child's speech or language skills, the next step is to determine who to call. In the United States, you have several options.

Private Practitioners

Private practitioners are usually located in the yellow pages under "Speech Pathologist." Some private speech pathologists will come to your home, but most have a professional office. You should ask to see the SLP's state license; although a national license from ASHA is not required, it is desirable.

Some advantages of using a private practioner include the following:

- *Convenience.* Flexible office hours or home visits make attending therapy sessions more convenient.
- *Specialized expertise.* For certain cases, a private speech-pathologist may have a specialty in your child's particular area,

especially in cases of stuttering, swallowing disorders, voice problems, or hearing impairment.

- *Personalized care.* Individualized treatment may allow children with serious problems to get more intensive and personalized therapy than in other settings. Communication with you is more frequent, since you will see the clinician each time your child attends.
- *Wider range of services.* Many schools do not provide services for mild articulation problems or tongue thrust. A private practitioner can work with your child to overcome this type of problem.

Some disadvantages of using a private practitioner include the following:

- *Cost.* Unless you have private insurance or are financially well-off, private speech therapy can be quite expensive, costing anywhere from $70 to $150 per hour for individual treatment. Always ask what the therapist charges before making an appointment.
- *Isolation from school.* A private practitioner is in a difficult position to work with your child's teachers on a consistent basis, which is very important if your child has serious language or listening problems.
- *Possible limited experience, materials, and comfort with children.* Since children are primarily served through the public schools, many private speech pathologists spend more time with adult patients. Their offices may be sterile and have limited materials for young children. Make sure the private practitioner is comfortable, experienced, and set up for working with children.

Public Schools

If your child attends the public schools, services are free. You pay taxes for the services provided in the public schools, so don't hesitate to use them. Children who attend private schools are also entitled to access to public school specialists on a limited basis. You should call your state's education department to find out your rights if your child attends a private school. In many states, public school speech-language pathologists have the same or greater training requirements as hospital or private practice SLPs. In this case, it is not a matter of "you get what you pay for."

Public schools now often provide evaluations and therapeutic services for children *before* they enter school. Call your local school system and ask for the Special Education Department to find out what services are offered.

Some advantages for using a public school speech-language pathologist include the following:

- *Experience, materials, and comfort with children.* Because public school SLPs deal with literally hundreds of children, they should be comfortable and proficient with diagnosing and treating children's speech and language problems. Also, they have access to a vast array of materials designed for children.
- *Access and availability to other professionals.* For infants and preschool-age children, the speech-language pathologist usually works as a member of a team. Your child will have access to their areas of expertise as well. The SLP can more easily work with the teachers to help your child function in the classroom successfully.
- *Cost.* It's free!

Some disadvantages of using a public school speech-language pathologist include the following:

- *Lack of time.* Many school systems are pinched due to staffing shortages and budget cuts. Large caseloads mean less time for planning lessons, working with students, and talking to you. Also, with so many school vacations, assemblies, and other interferences, therapy is sometimes not as consistent as in other settings.
- *Lack of individualization.* Because of the preceding issues, many school clinicians are forced to group children who, perhaps in ideal circumstances, might be better served individually or in a more appropriate group.
- *Red tape.* Getting help in a public school setting is often a bureaucratic process, requiring lots of forms, meetings, and waiting.

Hospitals

To find out if your local hospital can help you, call the general information number and ask whether there is a Speech Therapy Department. SLPs in a hospital setting are always state licensed and typically serve all age groups.

Some advantages of using a hospital-based speech-language pathologist include the following:

- *Access to technical equipment.* Hospitals have equipment on the premises that can be particularly useful when treating certain speech problems, such as hearing impairment, voice disorders, cleft palate, swallowing disorders, and stuttering.
- *Access to medical personnel.* This is particularly important to children with more involved cases, particularly children with head trauma, a cochlear implant, serious psychological or psychiatric issues, neurological and biological disorders, prenatal defects, and facial deformities.
- *Specialization.* In hospitals that cater strictly to children, you can find some of the leading experts on speech disorders related to medical conditions such as those just mentioned. Many times, research is conducted at teaching hospitals, which helps staff stay current with the latest breakthroughs in the field.

Some disadvantages of using a hospital speech-language pathologist include the following:

- *Cost.* Unless you have insurance, costs can be quite high. Always ask before making an appointment.
- *Isolation from school.* A hospital-based clinician, like the private practitioner, is in a difficult position to consult with a child's teachers on a consistent basis. Also, recommendations given are sometimes difficult to implement in a public school setting.
- *Limited experience, materials, and comfort with children.* Since children are primarily served through the public schools, many hospital speech pathologists spend more time with adult patients. However, in a children's hospital or large city hospital, this is not the case.

College Speech Clinics

To find out whether a college offers services that you need, call the general information number and ask whether there is a Speech and Hearing Department or Communication Sciences Department. The secretary in these departments can connect you with the professor who handles inquiries about the college speech therapy program, if there is one. A college with a student major in speech pathology will usually offer therapy services by trained students. A licensed SLP closely supervises the students, reviewing lesson plans, observing, and giving helpful suggestions.

Some advantages of using a student speech therapist from a college clinic include the following:

- *Cost.* In some cases, therapy costs may be reduced or eliminated for those with financial limitations. Regardless, fees are usually considerably less than what a private practitioner or hospital would charge.
- *Availability of services.* For many rural areas, a college speech clinic may be the only place a child can receive services.
- *Latest theory and practices utilized.* Because of the very nature of a college campus, professors are always looking at the most up-to-date information and research. Students have the benefit of their input and expertise.

Some disadvantages of using a student speech therapist from a college clinic include the following:

- *Lack of continuity.* Because students come and go from semester to semester or year to year, your child will have to reestablish a rapport with each new therapist. Also, the therapist needs time to get to know your child.
- *Inconvenience.* Most colleges have limited parking areas, so you may have to walk quite a distance with a young child in tow. Also, there is typically minimal flexibility as far as scheduling the sessions because the supervisor has to be present, or at least available.
- *Inexperience.* A student clinician brings extensive training to the therapy sessions, which should not be minimized. Also, many student clinicians have a natural "feel" for children and will do superior work. Nevertheless, they are still learning and may make some minor judgmental errors at times. Although good supervisors will be quick to remedy problems, they cannot be in all therapy rooms at one time and may not witness these moments.

Agencies

The term *agency* is somewhat broad. Sometimes an agency caters to children with specific problems such as cerebral palsy, mental retardation, deafness, or recovery from a brain injury. It can be a nonprofit, public, or private enterprise. Increasingly, if school systems are short-staffed, or are part of a regional program to service children under the age of 3 or 5 to comply with state or federal regulations, they are contracting out services to agencies. Typically, agencies provide a wide array of services, such as physical therapy and occupational therapy.

Some advantages of using an agency-based speech-language pathologist include the following:

- *Specialization.* Sometimes a speech therapist in this setting works predominantly with children having a specific set of problems, usually requiring specialized training. This focus is important if your child requires special attention.
- *Availability of other staff and services.* Because of its nature, an agency can coordinate services if your child requires them. This capacity cuts down on your running around and facilitates necessary teamwork.
- *Experience, materials, and comfort with children.* Like public school SLPs, agency-based clinicians deal with many children and so should be comfortable and proficient with diagnosing and treating your child's speech and language problems. Also, they have access to a vast array of materials designed for children.

Some disadvantages for using an agency-based speech-language pathologist include the following:

- *Isolation of skills.* If a child receives different kinds of therapy from several individuals, the program can become fragmented. It may be more helpful to receive therapy as part of one integrated "class." Many agencies don't offer this type of "school." Instead, specialists look at isolated parts of the child and work on their areas of specialty. For infants, this is not a problem, but as children reach the age of 3, a different approach may be appropriate.
- *Cost.* Cost varies from agency to agency. Even a nonprofit agency, however, needs to charge fees to cover expenses. If a school system has made arrangements for the services, you won't have to pay for them. For certain problems, insurance may pay. Ask first.
- *Scheduling and convenience.* This is particularly problematic if your child will have to attend therapy after school hours. Many children resent this and feel imposed upon. It also presents you with a lot of running around.

Appendix A at the back of this book lists the phone numbers of national organizations in the United States and Canada that can direct you to the appropriate, nationally licensed person or state association, if you are still unsure about where to call. This listing may be especially helpful for people in rural areas, where services can be sparse.

About Insurance Coverage

At this time, most health insurance companies do *not* cover expenses for a speech-language evaluation or therapy unless the problem is related to a medical condition or automobile accident. A doctor must make a referral for the initial evaluation and authorize treatment. Often the treatment is covered for a limited number of sessions or a fixed dollar amount. The American Speech-Language-Hearing Association is actively working to improve access to services and increase insurance coverage.

The Evaluation

Once you have decided *who* you want to perform the evaluation, you'll want to know *what* to expect when you make that first phone call. What happens during an evaluation? What should I tell my child? Read on to find out the answers to these and other questions you may have about the evaluation process.

The First Step: A Screening

Before a formal evaluation takes place, the SLP may want to meet your child and do some informal testing, called a *screening*. The screening determines whether an evaluation is necessary or not, and if so, which tests would be the most appropriate for the child. A screening can take anywhere from five to twenty minutes. The therapist may want to observe your child in a classroom or interacting with other classmates. In the public schools, some SLPs routinely perform screenings on all incoming kindergarten students and then again in a later, usually the second, grade. Children who have difficulty on this screening are typically monitored or referred for a complete evaluation. Permission from the parent for a screening may or may not be required, depending on the state and the nature of the screening. As a parent, you can (and should!) request a screening if you have any concerns at all about your child's communication skills. Since the word *test* often makes a child uncomfortable and tense before walking in the door, as with all phases of testing, your child need only be told that "Mr. or Ms. Smith would like to meet you and talk to you for a while." If the child should ask why, it usually suffices to say, "Because it is your turn."

The Legal Process

Once you or the SLP decides to pursue a full speech-language evaluation, a certain legal process must take place. (*Note:* You may choose to skip the screening and request a full evaluation from the beginning.) When the evaluation is to be performed through a public school system, a meeting may be required first. Some states simply require the parent or guardian's written permission for the evaluation in lieu of a meeting. This process is a result of legislative acts that established Public Laws 94–142 and 102–119, which are federal laws that guarantee special education services for those students who need them. Public schools consider speech-language therapy services a "special education" or "related service" and therefore follow this process.

You must be notified before a meeting that concerns your child is scheduled. If your state requires this meeting, you will be invited to hear the concerns leading to the evaluation. Usually the meeting will include a school administrator, specialists working with the child, teachers (if the child is in school), and the parents. Informal strategies that have been implemented to attempt to remediate the problem, if applicable, are discussed. You will be asked to sign formal permission papers allowing the speech-language evaluation to be done. If you cannot attend the meeting, the papers may be sent home for your signature. (If a parent does not speak English, an interpreter must be provided by the school system.) *If you do not grant written permission, an evaluation cannot be performed.* It is important to note that granting permission for the evaluation does not mean you have granted permission to begin therapy.

What Is the Speech-Language Pathologist Looking For?

The speech-language evaluation seeks to answer these questions:

- Is there a communication "problem"?
- What kind of problem is it?
- To what degree is the child impaired?
- Should other professionals be asked to do evaluations? For example: a referral to a psychologist, neurologist, or learning disabilities teacher.

- How does this problem affect the child on a day-to-day basis, at home and at school?
- If needed, what kind of intervention will best help this child?
- What can the parents (and teachers, if the child is school-age) do to help the child?

Informal and Formal Tests

Both **informal tests** and **formal tests** will be used to answer the preceding questions. Informal tests (or "tasks") are activities initiated by the speech-language pathologist for a specific purpose. The activities are not manufactured by an educational testing company, nor are they necessarily asked in a uniform way for each child. The speech-language pathologist knows how a typical child at a given age should respond to conversational questions.

For example, I often begin my evaluation by chatting with a student about any number of casual topics, such as what they were doing in class earlier that day. This may seem like a waste of time to an untrained observer, but this type of "chatting" gives a trained professional a great deal of insight as to how a child processes questions, stays on topic, articulates words, uses vocabulary, and puts sentences together. Following directions, telling stories, and describing pictures are other examples of informal tasks. Results are usually reported by noting the child's responses as "age appropriate" or, if the child had difficulty completing the task, more descriptively (i.e., "Johnny described the busy construction picture with minimal detail and awkward phrasing. He displayed similar syntax deficits in his conversational speech. Ex: 'I no want to have sausage on a pizza for lunch' ").

Formal tests refer to manufactured tests sold by companies that have developed a product. Data provided on a chart tell test givers what is a "typical" performance on a particular formal test. These *norms* are developed by giving the test to hundreds, and sometimes thousands, of children. The responses and performance of the typical 7-year-old children who took the test dictate what is expected (the "standard") for the 7-year-old child who takes the test once it is published. That is why formal tests are also called **standardized tests.**

What Will Happen during the Evaluation?

Most speech-language evaluations include a battery of tests that will take a half hour to three hours to administer, depending on the age of your child and the nature of the evaluation. Usually the evaluation is administered in several sessions instead of all at once. A combination of formal and informal tests will be used during the evaluation to provide a complete picture of the child's speech-language ability and use. The evaluation consists of the following components.

Background Information

The evaluator should discuss your concerns with you. The two of you will need to review your child's health and development as an infant and toddler. This developmental history is an important component of any evaluation. It helps identify any "red flag" areas such as delayed milestones for walking, a family history of language or learning problems, complications at birth, frequent ear infections, allergies, or other pertinent concerns that may signal a problem. The evaluator should also talk to your child's teacher, to see how the child is functioning in the classroom. Samples of your child's schoolwork as well as scores in past reading tests should be considered. *Any time a child is evaluated for a speech or language problem, the results of a recent hearing screening should be included in the background history.* The hearing screening can be done at the school by the school nurse, even if your child is not yet in school. If your child is under the care of an ear, nose, and throat doctor, these tests can be administered by an audiologist in the office, but you will have to pay for the tests.

Communication Skills in Other Settings

Your child should be observed in a natural setting such as at home, with other children, or in class. Is your child paying attention? Does she give body language to suggest she is confused? Does your child initiate conversation?

Receptive Language Skills

As discussed in earlier chapters, receptive language refers to what a child is able to understand. Receptive language is tested through a variety of pointing and direction-following activities that do not require children to speak. It determines if they understand words, sentences, or stories. Many children with speech or language problems have no difficulty comprehending what others are saying to them. Other children are confused by spoken language. They understand bits and pieces but miss the bigger picture, or vice versa. For example, when asked to point to a picture of "the girls are eating," Zeb, a child with a receptive language problem, pointed to a picture of one girl eating. He didn't realize what most children figure out without being directly or formally taught: that *girls* means more than one. When Zeb was asked to point to the "large brown circle," he chose a large red circle. What the speech therapist wants to find out is whether Zeb was never taught his colors, forgot them, or forgot the direction.

Expressive Language Skills

Testing of expressive language examines your child's spoken language. Age-appropriate use of word forms and endings (**morphology**), sentence structure (**syntax**) and word use (**semantics**) are examined. Additionally, how does your son or daughter put sentences together to retell a story? Can you follow the plot or is it confusing? Does your child use gestures or noises to be understood? Skills considered important to using language successfully in a school or in a social setting, such as answering open-ended and direct questions in a way that can be easily understood, are also considered.

Auditory Skills

Auditory skills refer to *how* your child hears what is said. Can your son or daughter remember and repeat what is said to him or her? Can your child listen to sounds (e.g., *c-a-t*) and figure out the word is *cat* when the sounds are put together? Can your child listen attentively to one voice when it is noisy in the background? These skills are particularly important to assess in school-age children because they are necessary for learning to read and following a discussion or lecture in a classroom setting.

Pragmatics

Pragmatics refers to the use of language that is appropriate to the situation. Does your child maintain eye contact when speaking and listening in a social situation? Are his words socially appropriate? Does your child frequently interrupt the conversation with unrelated stories or comments?

Metalinguistics

Metalinguistics refers to how well your child can talk about language. It is more appropriate to test these skills when your child is of school age. Does he know the difference between a sound, word, and a sentence? Can he listen to a sentence and break it down into individual words?

Articulation and Phonology

Articulation refers to how your child pronounces words. When children mispronounce a word because they don't understand the speech "rules" (as opposed to being physically unable to pronounce it, as with a simple articulation delay), they are facing a more pervasive problem called a **phonological disorder.** Why does a child pronounce the *s* perfectly in *sun* but leave it off on *snake?* Is there a pattern or reason for this? Does she pronounce words in an acceptable manner for her age? Is there a pattern to the problem? Does the problem carry over into reading and writing tasks?

Oral-Motor Function

An oral-motor exam checks the ability of the tongue, lips, and other muscles to move adequately for good speech production and swallowing. This is particularly necessary when a child displays difficulty pronouncing words or is late in starting to talk. The teeth should also be examined to ensure an adequate bite. In addition, the way your child swallows, with and without food, should be examined.

Voice Quality

The speech therapist should take notes on the quality of your child's voice. If a cold or a sore throat affects speech that day, your child should be checked on another day to make sure the voice returns to normal. Your child may be asked to perform informal tasks to analyze the voice quality at this stage. The speech therapist may administer some formal voice tests as well.

Fluency

Stuttering is called **dysfluency** by professionals in the field. Evaluating dysfluency is done by observing and analyzing a child's stuttering in many different speaking situations. The type of stuttering (repetitions, hesitations, etc.) and amount of stuttering are recorded. Struggling behaviors such as grimacing or clenching of the fists are noted as well. Formal tests may be used.

Critical Thinking and Reasoning Skills

This refers to problem-solving skills and a child's ability to find and explain solutions to problems. Can your child understand a cause and effect relationship? Does she analyze what is heard and draw conclusions or form opinions?

For most children, a combination of the preceding areas should be examined, depending on the individual's needs.

Special Considerations:
Testing Infants and Preschoolers

Infants generally are evaluated through informal testing, which consists of observing and playing with them in different settings (with a parent, with toys, food, etc.) and noting what they do. Does your baby make any noise? Does she seem to anticipate the objects you present or even notice them? Does your baby look at you? The other important part of the evaluation is the interview with you, because you can answer questions about the baby's habits, development, and medical history. Watching your baby eat is another important part of the evaluation, because the examiner can watch how your baby's "talking muscles" work when she is eating.

Tests given to preschoolers are often a combination of formal and informal tests. The formal tests are designed to accommodate the shorter attention span and limited skills a young child possesses. You may be present in the room during the testing, but often a child responds better when the parent is close by but out of sight. Evaluators will let you know what their preferred practice is. The activities are often more "hands-on" and less clinical. As mentioned previously, to keep your child relaxed, avoid discussing the testing ahead of time or using the word *test* to describe what will happen. As far as your son or daughter needs to know, he or she is going to "play with" some new people.

A team, rather than an individual, often does the testing for this age group. This team assesses speech and language as well as other developmental skills, such as basic concepts, attention span, socialization skills, self-help skills, balance, coordination, and muscle tone. Members of the team should include a speech-language pathologist, occupational therapist and/or physical therapist, and special education teacher. A psychologist can also add invaluable insight into diagnosis and program development. Because delays in infants and preschool children are often not isolated to speech and language problems, team assessment offers a host of benefits. The other specialists can observe deficits in areas in which the speech therapist is not properly trained. These delays are often difficult to detect and often go unnoticed by the parents as well.

After the SLP's evaluation comes the report, filled with data and terminology you may have trouble interpreting. The next chapter will help translate the report for you. Chapter 4 will also help you plan the best treatment program for your daughter or son, in partnership with the appropriate professionals.

4

After the Evaluation: Understanding Report Jargon and the IEP

Once the speech-language pathologist (SLP) has performed the actual evaluation, it will either be discussed with you at that time, or you will be asked to come in and discuss the results at a later date. In either case, the SLP should send a written report within a few weeks. If you are not given a written report detailing the results of the evaluation, however, request one. Although not always required, most speech pathologists will gladly provide it.

In this chapter, I explain the meanings of the figures and special terminology you'll likely see in the speech pathologist's report. Specialists will commonly speak and write about your child with percentiles, age equivalents, standard deviations, and stanines. This professional jargon can be daunting if you have not studied it before. I also describe the legal process that takes place after the school evaluation, that is, the formal and necessary paperwork. Depending on your child's age and communication problem, different treatment options are usually suggested. I'll help you know what to anticipate, what questions to ask, and what role you'll be required to play. Finally, I detail the options for speech and language therapy that may be available for your son or daughter, so you'll know what to expect and what choices you'll be able to make.

The Numbers Used to Measure Performance

As we discussed in chapter 3, a speech-language therapist uses informal tasks (sometimes called informal tests) or formal tests (sometimes called standardized tests) to evaluate a child.

Standardized tests provide charts that indicate what is typical or expected performance in various skill areas at each age. The therapist then indicates how a particular child performed in comparison to a typical child of the same age. These comparisons can be expressed in percentiles, standard scores, standard deviations, stanines, and age equivalents. Many tests have charts to supply information in several of these ways. It's no wonder parents find reports to be so confusing!

You don't need to become an expert in testing statistics to understand these numbers. Nearly all tests use percentiles and/or age equivalents as the primary measure of performance. The other numbers provide additional systems for interpreting the data. If you become familiar and comfortable with percentiles and age equivalents, you should be able to understand most reports.

Percentiles: What They Mean

Percentiles, also called **percentile ranks,** are sometimes abbreviated on reports as "%tile." Most achievement scores are provided as percentiles and are particularly helpful in comparing the performance of one child to others in the same age group (or sometimes, the same grade). Percentiles range from 1 to 99 and can usually be interpreted as follows:

95–99	far superior to peers
75–95	exceeds the average performance
60–75	on the higher end of average
40–60	average
25–40	on the lower end of average
15–25	below average (may need help)
1–15	low (needs help)

Schools and other institutions with speech-language programs establish their own criteria as to how far below average a child must be to qualify for services. For example, all children scoring at or below the 20th, or even 10th, percentile may be considered deficient enough to be considered "handicapped" in a particular language area. This inconsistency among school districts can present a dilemma when a child moves from one school system to another.

It's important to note that the overwhelming majority of children will score between the 25th and 75th percentile on any given standardized test. Percentiles are not the same as a *percentage,* which is the number you may remember scoring on a test as a child that indicates the percentage of correct answers. Percentiles do not tell you how many questions were answered incorrectly.

For example, a 5-year-old child may only need to answer five of a given 15 questions correctly to be considered within the "average" (or "normal") range, because the questions are difficult. The same 15 questions may be asked of a 7-year-old. At age 7, perhaps eight questions would need to be answered correctly to be considered within normal limits. The number of "correct" answers increases with age. (If those responses were scored as traditional percentages, the 5-year-old would receive a score of 30 percent, which would sound like a failing score, where in reality, the percentile score translates to the 63rd percentile, which is well within the average range.)

The actual percentile number, 65 for example, indicates your child scored better than 65 percent of the children who took the same test. In essence, a score of 65 means your child's performance is in the top 35 percent of all the children who took the test. The speech-language pathologist is primarily concerned with your child's development in terms of what is normal for other children of the same age. That is why percentiles are an excellent tool to determine this comparison.

Age Equivalents

Though your child's actual **chronological age** may be 7-4 (7 years, 4 months), his performance or **age equivalent** (sometimes abbreviated as AE) may be comparable to a younger, 5-3 child (5 years, 3 months) on any given formal test. These scores are also given in years and months in the same way as a chronological age. The score means your child performed at the level of a child of the age given.

Standard Scores

Standard scores (sometimes abbreviated as SS) are based on a system in which 100 is the average score. Any score within 15 points on either side of 100 (85–115) is considered within the higher and lower ends of average. Scores lower than 85 are below average; scores above 115, above average. IQ tests are typically reported using standard scores, but language and auditory tests sometimes use this system as well.

Standard Deviation

Each test determines its own measure of what constitutes a **standard deviation (SD)**. The professional who administers the test has that information in the manual accompanying the test. Standard deviations measure how far from average (otherwise known as the "mean") a child scores. "One standard deviation below the mean," written as -1 SD, is below average. But that does not necessarily mean it is low enough to qualify the child for a remedial program. Likewise, any standard deviations above the mean would be considered an above-average performance. For example, one standard deviation above the mean would be written as $+1$ SD.

Most specialists use two or more standard deviations below the mean as the criteria to qualify for remediation. This is typically written as -2 SD.

Stanines

Stanines are based on a system from 1 to 9. Five is considered average. A stanine rating of 1 or 2 indicates a below-average performance. A stanine rating of 8 or 9 indicates an above-average performance. If you multiply a stanine by 10, it will give you a ballpark equivalent of a percentile.

What Happens after the Evaluation?

If your child was evaluated through the U.S. public schools, a second meeting will usually be scheduled to discuss the results of the evaluation and discuss recommendations. A school administrator should be present at this meeting, as well as any teacher or professional who works with your child.

The IEP and IFSP

A plan called an **Individualized Educational Program (IEP)** is developed by the team at the meeting following the evaluation. A signed IEP is a legally binding document, meaning the school system *must provide* the program it has promised. Parents are equal members of this planning team; they have the right to express opinions as to what service their child receives, how often, where it takes place, and what is learned. For children age 3 and younger, this plan is called an **Individualized Family Service Plan (IFSP).** *As the parent of the child, you hold many rights, and with them, the ultimate responsibility. If you do not grant written permission to begin therapy as specified on the IEP or IFSP, therapy cannot take place.*

The following are some questions that should be addressed at this meeting with the school team. If these areas are not discussed, be sure to ask!

- How do these speech and language deficits impact my child's academic performance?
- What modifications should be made in the classroom to minimize the impact of these deficits?
- What is the most appropriate learning environment for my child?
- How can my child's communication skills be strengthened within the classroom?
- How can I foster these skills at home?
- How do these speech, language, or listening deficits affect my child socially and emotionally?

By looking at the bigger picture, an educational program can be tailored to your child's individual needs as much as possible. It is important that your child is challenged to meet new, yet obtainable, educational goals.

The IEP and IFSP, by U.S. law, must include the following information:

- A description of your child's present level of functioning and diagnosis
- The goals of the therapy program
- How often therapy will take place
- Which professional(s) will carry out the program
- Where therapy will be provided (usually a regular classroom, resource room, or therapy room)
- Whether the therapy will be one-on-one or in a group
- What methods and materials will be used
- The criteria for being released from the program

In Canada, each province has complete autonomy when it comes to providing speech-language therapy and educational services. Unlike the United States, Canada does not have national laws that dictate how this is to be carried out. However, local school boards must provide appropriate programs for children with "exceptionalities." Speech and language are considered "communication exceptionalities." A report and program will be prepared for your child by the school, or speech pathologist, if handled through the Ministry of Health. There is no national standard for what information this report must provide. The school may or may not choose to provide the services of a speech-language pathologist, since this is often considered a health issue. Unlike U.S. schools, Canadian schools are not required to have speech pathologists on staff or available, and many don't. The classroom teacher and other learning specialists often take courses so that they can better help their students develop language and listening skills. Some provinces provide financial incentives to local school boards to secure specialists such as speech-language pathologists or psychologists. As in the United States, if you disagree with the recommendations, you can appeal the program that has been recommended in this report.

Modifications in the Educational Program

Additionally, because the IEP and IFSP are legal documents required by law for the purposes of individualizing a child's educational program, any **modification** in the child's educational program should be listed on these documents. Changes in the modifications should be made only with your knowledge and consent. Modifications describe what the teacher needs to do differently to accommodate your child's special needs to help him function successfully in the classroom. By law, any modifications written into the IEP *must* be followed by the classroom teacher; it is not a choice. Most IEPs, however, give the teacher some flexibility in how the modifications are carried out.

Modifications are invaluable and necessary, because they allow a child to compensate for a particular weakness. Appropriate modifications can mean the difference between a child who functions at top potential and thus enjoys school, and a child with lowered self-esteem who dreads school because of certain deficits. No child deserves to be overwhelmed by the educational system on a day-to-day basis through no fault of her own.

Some examples of typical modifications for children with language disorders follow. Teachers can do the following:

- Write directions and assignments on the board (for students with auditory memory problems)
- Speak at a slower rate (for students with auditory memory or language processing deficits)

- Give the child time to think and mentally organize before expecting a verbal response (for students with expressive language deficits such as word retrieval problems or sequencing difficulties)
- Provide written tests instead of oral tests (for students with auditory memory or processing deficits)
- Use multiple-choice or "word bank" test formats instead of fill-in-the-blank format (for students with word retrieval deficits or spelling deficits)
- Simplify, paraphrase, and prioritize oral and written information to be learned by the child (for students with receptive language deficits or language processing deficits)
- Exempt students from annual standardized tests or allow untimed tests (for students with a receptive or expressive language deficit whose skills are better evaluated individually)

Modifications: Unfair Special Treatment?

A language or listening disorder is a handicapping condition that often affects a person's ability to perform successfully in school in many subject areas. In the past few years, speech and language professionals have become more aware of the profound need, and use for, combining therapy with classroom modifications. National laws require students to be educated in the "least restrictive environment"; this means that special education students should not be taught in segregated classrooms unless all other options have been tried and failed. Most children with language disorders should have some type of modification in their day-to-day academic programs to enable them to keep up with their nonhandicapped peers.

Modifications are not cheating, nor are they unfair to the other children in the classroom. After all, the other children do not have the burden of living with a communication disorder. Do eyeglasses give a child with a visual deficit an unfair advantage? Does a child with a hearing aid have an unfair advantage? Of course not. These are the tools that help them play on a level playing field. So it is for a child with a language disorder. Unfortunately, these disorders cannot be detected by the eye or untrained ear, and so may not be perceived in the compassionate manner they should.

If you are concerned about your child being "singled out" for extra help or modifications, remember this: Because of the large number of children with IEP programs in schools today (typically 8 to 15 percent), children are accustomed to other students having slightly different assignments or tests and being helped by other teachers in and out of the classroom. It is nothing out of the ordinary in today's school.

Consultation Time

Consultation time refers to the number of minutes per week a specialist will spend with your child's classroom teacher or team of teachers to discuss topics such as therapy goals and modifications. Since modifications are vital to most children with language disorders, guidance of and collaboration with your child's teachers are important to make sure the recommendations are understood and carried out as intended, and adjusted properly when appropriate. Scheduled consultation time is relatively new for most speech-language pathologists who, in years past, operated in isolation. Today, speech-language pathologists are not only encouraged but expected to act as consultants in the public schools.

An individualized special education program must be constantly evaluated by the teachers and specialists in order to ensure things are going smoothly. Sometimes a child starts having difficulty keeping up with peers when the class begins a certain project or difficult chapter. This calls for creative solutions, which differ from child to child.

No standard exists for determining the amount of minutes needed per week for consultation. Obviously, children with a greater degree of handicap require more consultation time and creativity with programming. A reasonable amount of time can range from 10 to 15 minutes monthly for a child with minimal problems, to 30 minutes a week for a more challenged child.

Unfortunately, due to budget cuts, fewer staff members are available to go around. Time for consultation may be at a premium and squeezed in during lunch periods or before school. This is less desirable, but not always controllable.

Options for Speech and Language Therapy

It is important to know there are no hard and fast rules, professionally or legally, as to how often a child receives therapy or in what manner. These issues are determined on a case-by-case basis, depending on the needs of your child, your wishes, and scheduling issues for your child and the professionals who will be providing assistance.

Individual or Group Therapy?

Individual therapy is beneficial in some cases, particularly when a child's problem is unique or severe or when an appointment simply cannot be scheduled at another time. However, in other cases, group therapy may be helpful and more productive. The trick with group therapy is to make sure the members of the group are compatible, although not necessarily working on the same skills. For example, a fifth-grade boy should not be scheduled with a group of kindergarten and first-graders regardless of what skills he needs to work on. It simply would be degrading for him and awkward for the other students. Also, children in school need to be scheduled in a way that won't take them away from an important subject area, so this may limit scheduling and grouping options, thus resulting in small groups or individual sessions.

Speech-Language Therapy in the Classroom

Often parents worry their children will be ostracized for leaving the class- room to receive special help. Today it is not uncommon for children to leave the room throughout the day for a variety of programs and services. Lately, however, the trend has been toward trying to provide services of all kinds within the classroom walls, so the child's day and program are not too fragmented. This is particularly true and beneficial for children receiving several different types of special help. You might consider the following issues when deciding what is best for your child.

Team Teaching

Some speech-language pathologists now go into the classroom and work with children by "team teaching" with the classroom teacher on a peri- odic basis. This shows the classroom teacher how to structure speech and language lessons in the most effective way and provides an oppor- tunity for the child receiving therapy to reinforce skills learned in therapy in the classroom. In other team-teaching situations, the lessons are planned by both the classroom teacher and the speech-language pa- thologist and are carried out by both professionals. For example, after the classroom teacher introduces the lesson, the speech-language pa- thologist takes over the discussion portion of the lesson to maximize the involvement of those students who have specific speech and language goals. Team teaching involves the entire class, not just students with spe- cial needs.

Research has not been done to document whether this approach is more effective in addressing a child's speech and language needs than the traditional "pull-out" therapy program. For a child demonstrating a specific moderate or severe deficit in speech or language (with a normal IQ), I would not recommend a team-teaching approach as the complete program unless the classroom teacher has some special training in this area and is able to teach and reinforce needed skills throughout the day.

On the other hand, children with Down syndrome and other forms of mental retardation often do well with a team-teaching approach, improving their speech and language by imitating the other typical children's speech with a minimal amount of direct therapy. Children with lower IQs benefit from this approach (ASHA, 1993), because they learn better in everyday, natural settings as opposed to a clinical, "isolated" setting. If a mentally retarded child has a specific speech or language problem, however, individual or group therapy may also be very appropriate, if not necessary.

For children with autism, many social language (pragmatic) goals are well suited for being introduced in the classroom setting rather than in isolation. Also, for children with listening disorders, team teaching can be a very effective way of addressing a variety of listening skill goals.

In general, my experience has shown that team teaching is appropriate (and often ideal) for students with mild problems or certain types of language or listening weaknesses. However, team teaching alone does not provide enough individualization or opportunities for responses from children with more serious or specific problems, particularly in the area of articulation. Also, the classroom teacher cannot be expected to substitute for a professionally trained speech-language pathologist or have time to provide speech therapy to several children in a class of 25 or more.

In-Class Therapy

With preschool and young elementary students, having the speech-language pathologist come into the classroom to provide therapy to individuals or small groups can be more easily accommodated, if not preferred, at times. Children with mild problems or who are working on integrating previously learned skills can benefit from in-class lessons. Children who have pragmatic language (social use of language) delays also benefit from working on these skills in the classroom setting. Classrooms with several children needing services provide an excellent opportunity for the speech-language pathologist to group students and utilize interactive games. When therapy is provided in the class, only those students who have identified speech, language, and listening problems typically receive direct services.

Conducting therapy sessions in the class, however, is limiting as far as the nature of the lessons conducted. For example, music and movement activities, which are helpful with younger children, would be distracting to the other students. Likewise, some oral-motor exercises require the blowing of horns or bubbles, which cannot be done in a classroom where other lessons are taking place. Children who need to work on exercises for their lips and tongue may feel embarrassed to do so within view of their classmates. Children who are working on certain listening skills may need a quiet room with minimal distractions, particularly in the early stages of their therapy program. Children who are working on speech skills also need to speak at a normal conversational level so that the speech pathologist can hear whether they are pronouncing the words correctly. When a teacher is trying to conduct a lesson, this can be distracting for the child, teacher, and class. Thus, in many cases, in-class therapy is simply not the most practical way to provide services.

Some parents prefer this in-class therapy so that their child does not have to feel awkward going for special help. However, with this arrangement, the rest of the child's classmates see the therapy taking place right in the classroom, which sometimes draws perhaps even more attention to the child. It is important to weigh all the issues when deciding where the therapy should take place. Most schools do try to accommodate a parent's wishes in this regard if appropriate or feasible.

Therapy with Private Practitioners, Hospitals, and Clinics

If you take your child to see a private-practice speech-language pathologist or one in a hospital or clinic, you can expect your child will be asked to attend sessions once or twice per week, for 30 to 60 minutes per session. This may be increased or reduced as needed and may be on an individual or small-group basis.

The therapist who works with your child should give you suggestions for ways to reinforce at home the skills taught in the sessions. Additionally, if your child is of school age, the child's teacher should be made aware that she is receiving this help. The therapist should be encouraged to communicate with the teacher, either through reports or telephone calls, about the nature of the therapy and in what way the teacher can help. It is also a good idea to inform the school's speech-language pathologist, so he or she knows the child's needs are being addressed.

Therapy in U.S. Public Schools

In the public school system, the services offered to children with speech and language problems vary as far as what therapy is provided, as well as where it is provided, according to the age of the child and the child's needs.

Public School Therapy Programs for Children under 5 Years Old

Young children's speech, language, and listening development can be addressed in a variety of ways, depending on their unique needs. Again, there is no one right way to provide therapy or help.

If your child is under the age of 3, a speech-language pathologist can be contacted through the school and will typically work with you in your home or have you bring your son or daughter to a location for therapy. Sometimes therapy may be done on a monthly basis. For this age, the SLP helps you and other caregivers in your family learn to provide stimulation to your infant to facilitate development. In special cases, such as hearing impairment (particularly with a cochlear-implanted child) or cleft palate, therapy may be more direct and frequent. Again, the child's needs have to be considered.

If your child is between the ages of 3 and 5, intervention is typically provided through actual therapy sessions at a local public school or as part of a preschool program. The therapist may go into the preschool classroom and work with your child or the whole class in order to address speech and language development skills. Many schools now set up their own preschool classes, several mornings or afternoons per week, to address the needs of their local children with special needs. Preschoolers with no learning problems are often included in these programs in many communities. This helps the special needs students by allowing them to see children their own age setting good examples. Typical children benefit as well, because they are provided with a preschool program (sometimes at no cost) with much smaller classes and more teachers than a traditional preschool program. Many states are encouraging and funding such programs in response to recent changes in the federal law and past successes.

Public School Therapy Programs for Elementary School Children

Once your child has reached kindergarten, speech and language therapy is provided in many different ways.

For mild speech and language problems, you might expect the following:

1. Individual or group therapy sessions, if needed at all, may be held once a week or even less frequently. Therapy may instead be concentrated in your child's classroom or in a "speech room." Another alternative is the team teaching or consultative approach described earlier in this chapter.
2. The therapist will communicate regularly with you and the classroom teacher.
3. Your child's progress in speech, language, and listening, as well as in other academic areas such as reading, will be monitored.

For moderate to severe speech and language problems, you might expect the following:

1. Individual or group therapy sessions may be held two or more times a week. This may take place in your child's classroom, therapy room, learning or resource center, or a combination of places.
2. Team teaching when possible and/or joint planning sessions (called consultation) will be conducted with your child's classroom teacher and any other specialists working with your child, to plan lessons and strategies that would be beneficial for his speech and language development within the curriculum being taught. This may be necessary on a weekly basis for some children and should be written right into the IEP if it is expected. As mentioned previously, however, many schools are suffering from shortages of speech-language pathologists and may have difficulty working weekly consultation times into the schedule.
3. The therapist will provide regular communication, and, if appropriate, follow-up activities you can do at home to improve your son or daughter's speech and language skills.

Public School Therapy Programs for the Adolescent

As your child enters middle or junior high school, new issues arise. You, the speech therapist, and classroom teachers must weigh priorities and examine your child's progress in therapy. Is your child still improving? Does your child resist going to therapy or doing the recommended home activities? Is your child feeling overwhelmed with all the responsibilities and changes of middle school? These questions are valid to ask at any age, but they become particularly necessary once your child leaves elementary school. If your child still has a language or listening disorder (it can be assumed to be a permanent problem if it has continued to this age), it should be discussed at a joint meeting with you, the speech pathologist, and all teachers involved. If changes (modifications) in the way teachers present lessons and/or tests are needed for your child to succeed, these should be discussed and written into the IEP, regardless of whether your child receives direct therapy.

The following are some reasons that therapy may *not* be appropriate at this age:

1. Adolescents may resist going for help and, therefore, are poor candidates for therapy.
2. Scheduling demands often create problems. A student may adamantly refuse to leave a class in which he does well in order to attend therapy sessions, although the student logically should miss that one rather than a class that is more challenging. With many teachers involved, there is less flexibility during the day.
3. Progress may have reached a "plateau." The fact is, there are some students who will always have a speech, language, or listening problem. Once compensation strategies have been taught, isolated exercises and therapy may be of little use by this age, particularly for children with language or listening disorders.
4. Students with other learning disabilities may need to focus their attention on succeeding in the classroom, which may leave little time or energy for attending separate classes or completing separate homework assignments. Again, prioritizing your child's needs is the key.

Remember, there is no one single right way to plan a student's speech, language, and listening program. Many adolescents continue to attend speech and language classes in middle and senior high school and continue to improve. If your son or daughter continues to make steady progress and does not resist attending therapy or language classes, I recommend continuing your child in the program, even at the middle or high school level. Many schools are trying to find innovative ways to involve the speech-language pathologist in the classroom and make the goals and activities more functional and meaningful for those students who need special help.

PART II
Speech, Language, and Listening Problems

5

Understanding Speech Problems

Speech problems often trouble parents far more than children. If children can speak well enough to be understood, especially at a young age, they are usually satisfied. But as a parent, it can be unnerving to hear your child stutter or ask for a "wewwow cwayon," like an old Elmer Fudd cartoon. "Oh no," you may think. "I remember Jimmy Wesner talking like that in 11th grade. People used to make fun of him. I don't want anyone to make fun of *my* child."

In your heart, you may know it's probably something that your child will outgrow in a few years. After reading the first few chapters of this book, you may be even more reassured. Yet, just waiting and *hoping* is a tall order for any parent, I know. Always remember that a speech, language, or listening problem is only a very small part of who your child is. It does not define your child.

Things have changed dramatically since Jimmy Wesner was in school. Chances are Jimmy Wesner never had the opportunity to have speech therapy, because U.S. national laws requiring schools to provide it were only enacted in 1975. In addition, U.S. laws requiring that schools provide preschool speech therapy were only passed in the early 1990s. Because of these laws and changing attitudes toward disabilities and differences of all kinds, children today are exposed to many people their age who are different from them. By the time they reach 11th grade, seeing someone who looks, acts, or speaks differently should be far less unusual for your child than for earlier generations.

In this chapter, I give you a crash course on the most common speech problems. I explain the nature of and treatment for stuttering, pronunciation problems, and voice problems. For each one, I describe the characteristics of the problem, how a child is affected, and what you as a parent can do to help your son or daughter.

It is not necessary for you to become an expert in the field, but by becoming better informed, you will have a greater understanding of your child and her unique needs.

Stuttering

M-m-mom? C-c-can I go over to-to-to Billy's house? I-I-I . . . I will be back after lunch. Wha-Wha-Whaaat are we having for lunch?
—Jamie, age 6

We've all had problems tripping over words before. If you pay close attention when you talk today, I bet you'll find yourself repeating words. In fact, "stuttering" is a normal part of everyday conversation. Speech requires quite a bit of coordination between the mouth, vocal cords, and brain. Sometimes one is moving a little faster than the other, and-uh-and we stutter. But what makes our normal, everyday repetitions of words different from those of a person with a true stuttering problem? In this section you will learn how to recognize and understand a child with Jamie's problem and what can be done for children like him.

When children learn to talk, they go through a normal "phase" in which they repeat words or phrases. For example, "Mommy, Mommy, look at-look at that!" It sounds and looks a lot like stuttering. This usually happens between the ages of about 2 and 5. Sometimes the child does this for a few days; other times it lasts for months or even a few years, even though the child does not have a stuttering problem. The key to distinguishing between a normal phase and a true stuttering problem is how often the child stutters and in what way.

Diagnosis and Causes of Stuttering

A child who stutters is said to be *dysfluent.* Although diagnosing the difference between a normal stuttering phase and a true dysfluent speech pattern is tricky business in the preschool years, there are some specific indicators that a speech-language pathologist will examine. For example, stutterers like Jamie tend to get stuck on the first sound of a word, often the first word in a sentence. They may repeat the first sound or syllable several times, instead of just once or twice. Once they get the word out, stutterers tend to speak very quickly, as though in a mad rush to finish before getting stuck again. Jamie knows what he wants to say. The hesitancy in his speech happens when the word gets stuck in his throat, not because he needs time to collect his thoughts.

Stuttering usually begins gradually, by the time the child is about age 5. But sometimes the only way to be sure that a child has a stuttering problem is to watch what happens over time to see if it gets better or worse.

To diagnose stuttering, the therapist observes the child talking in a number of situations and takes careful notes as to how many times the child exhibits stuttering behaviors; the therapist also notes whether the child shows frustration. Some behaviors that show frustration are stamping feet, clenching fists, blinking eyes, or grimacing. Standardized tests and informal methods for diagnosing and rating stuttering exist as well. Typically, a combination of both is used to diagnose a dysfluent child.

What causes stuttering? Quite simply, there is currently no clear answer. In years past, stuttering was thought to be primarily a psychological problem. Although we do know that anxiety can make stuttering worse, we now also know that there is much more to the story. Some researchers theorize that stuttering has a physiological basis or that a child is genetically predisposed toward stuttering (Kidd, 1977), but we really do not know why it happens in some children and not in others. It is entirely possible that stuttering has multiple causes.

Characteristics of Children with Stuttering Problems

Children with stuttering problems might do the following:

- Repeat the initial sound in a word ("Sh-sh-she is nice.")
- Repeat parts of words ("Mis-mis-mister Jones is here.")
- Prolong the initial sound in a word ("M———ommy's home.")
- Say "I can't say it!" or "I can't get it out!"
- Hesitate before talking, although they appear to be ready to say something (". . . I want some juice.")
- Get stuck on the first word in a thought or phrase
- Rush the rest of the sentence once a word that was stuck is spoken
- Open their mouths with no sound coming out when trying to talk

- Grimace when trying unsuccessfully to talk
- Show frustration by blinking, stamping feet, or clenching fists

How Does Stuttering Affect a Child?

A stuttering problem can be very frustrating for a child. But as with every speech, language, and listening problem, each child will respond to the frustration in his or her own way. Some may cope by avoiding speaking situations and becoming "shy." Sometimes children who are unresponsive to speech therapy have other anxieties or issues unrelated to the stuttering that "fuel the fire" of stuttering. For those children, dealing with the underlying causes of stress through counseling may help them benefit from speech therapy. Any kind of stress or excitement may aggravate a stuttering problem, which is why holidays, birthdays, and beginning a new school year are particularly difficult times for a child who stutters. Likewise, certain situations, such as talking on the telephone or speaking in front of an audience, can sometimes be troublesome for children who stutter. They may avoid talking in those situations because of associations with past stuttering incidents. Sometimes certain words trigger a fear of stuttering for the same reason, and the child may find creative ways to avoid using those words. Because fear can propel a child who stutters into a more pronounced stuttering episode, the child will avoid situations or words that induce fear. The speech pathologist will help the child gain confidence in nonthreatening speaking situations before approaching the child's personal fear-inducing words or situations.

In my experience, however, children who stutter are frequently not overly self-conscious or inhibited about speaking, especially at a younger age. This is particularly true if their parents are relaxed and tolerant of the stuttering. Sometimes adults are so conscious of how they look and act around other people that they assume a child will feel the same way. But many children who stutter have learned to accept their differences and express themselves quite openly and readily. Your reactions to a child who stutters will send one of two messages to the child: either you are interested in what the child has to say *or* you are impatient and distracted by the stuttering. Children who feel their message is valued will tend to want to talk more and not let the stuttering stop them.

As far as how stuttering affects a child's academic performance, there is no research that indicates any relationship between the two.

Therapy for a Child Who Stutters

There are many philosophies regarding stuttering therapy. Previously, most therapists took a "wait and see" attitude with preschool stutterers and deferred formal therapy until a child was of elementary school age. Today, however, more therapists initiate intervention at an earlier age and find success. Usually a child is monitored for a period of time, perhaps six months, to see whether a sporadic or recent problem becomes a more consistent, long-term problem. For example, before beginning formal speech therapy, the speech pathologist may give the parent some suggestions for facilitating a conducive speaking environment for the child at home. If the stuttering behaviors do not change, or they worsen, formal therapy may be initiated, even in the preschool years.

Do children "grow out" of the problem if nothing is done? Perhaps some will. In fact, as many as 80 percent of stutterers do eventually stop stuttering without help. The reasons for this are as mysterious as what causes stuttering.

Speech therapy is designed to improve a child's **fluency.** For a severe stutterer, intensive therapy several times a week may be helpful, particularly in the beginning. As the child gains more confidence and control in speaking situations, the frequency of the sessions can be reduced. Although some children completely stop stuttering after attending therapy, speech therapy is not a cure. Rather, it gives the child strategies to minimize the stuttering blocks and teaches special breathing and relaxation techniques to keep speech flowing more fluently. For many stutterers, this requires constant conscious thought when speaking; that is, they cannot always talk freely without focusing on these strategies. For many others, however, these strategies become second nature. There also are some stutterers who, for some reason, do not respond to speech therapy despite their best efforts.

What Can Parents Do to Help a Child Who Stutters?

Your child's speech pathologist will undoubtedly have specific activities for you to regularly practice and "play" with your child. How often you should practice and which activities you should do will depend on the age of your child, the nature and degree of the stuttering problem, and the therapy method being used. However, some general guidelines are applicable to all children who stutter. Here are some ways to help if your child has been diagnosed with a stuttering problem:

- Speak to your child in a calm, slow, relaxed voice.
- Keep stress and conflict in the home to a minimum.
- Let your child finish speaking, no matter how long it takes, without interrupting.

- After your child speaks, pause before you respond.
- Avoid drawing attention to your child's stuttering.
- Do not insist that your child repeat mispronounced words or grammatically incorrect sentences. Instead, simply rephrase what your child said using correct grammar and pronunciation; for example, if the child says, "Jenny not g-g-going," you can say, "That's right. Jenny *isn't* going."
- Avoid putting your child on the spot by making him answer questions or talk in front of an audience of relatives or friends.

Case Study: Jenna

Jenna transferred into our second grade in January. Her mother called me right away to let me know Jenna had been receiving speech therapy in her previous school system. "She was doing pretty well for the last year or so," she told me. "We even thought about discontinuing speech therapy. But the last few weeks have been pretty rough. Jenna can hardly get a word out without a struggle. I hope we haven't made a big mistake with this move. What should we do?"

I spoke with Jenna's teacher, who also was concerned about her stuttering. We worked out a therapy schedule at Jenna's IEP (Individualized Educational Plan) meeting. Jenna would begin with speech therapy three times a week to help get her back on track, then once or twice a week once she was speaking fluently 85 percent of the time. The decision regarding when to reduce Jenna's speech time would be made at a later meeting with Jenna's mother, teacher, and myself.

I assured Jenna's mother this was probably just a short-term setback for her and was not unexpected under the circumstances. Although the move might have aggravated Jenna's stuttering for the moment, Jenna's mother and father certainly could not be blamed for her stuttering problem. I pointed out that Jenna would have other sources of stress throughout her life and might have future lapses as well. We would work together to help Jenna get control of her fluency again.

In about three months, Jenna began gradually to speak with more fluency. I spoke with her therapist from her previous school, who was happy to share with me strategies she had tried with success, as well as those that were not helpful. Jenna's therapy focused on her breathing and speech patterns. We tackled troublesome words and situations gradually, after meeting success with easier words and phrases. By the end of Jenna's second-grade year, she was speaking with about 80–85 percent fluency. When she was excited or upset, her speech would be less fluent.

Jenna is now in eighth grade and was phased out of speech therapy in sixth grade. Her mother reports that she is usually fluent but does have moments of struggling from time to time. When that happens, Jenna uses the strategies she learned in speech therapy to help her work through the block.

Common Pronunciation Problems

Most of the time I can figure out what Ben wants from us. We've developed a "code" if you will. For example, I know when he says "gogga" he wants me to take him in the car somewhere. I feel bad when other people don't understand him, but we've learned to be good translators. It's not a problem for us, so why bother subjecting him to speech therapy? I wouldn't want him to feel like he's different from the other kids. Besides, I heard that most kids outgrow this stuff. If he doesn't, they can work with him when he gets to kindergarten.
—Father of Ben, age 4

Unfortunately, Ben is probably painfully aware of how different his speech sounds from that of his friends. He is most likely frustrated at his inability to be understood and may resent the need for Mom and Dad to act as interpreters. His speech is a problem. When a child's speech is a problem, adults must reach out and get the help needed. Though time does do wonders for most children, for some it just adds up to prolonged frustration and embarrassment.

Knowing which problem your child will grow out of and which will continue to be a problem may be impossible for you to determine, even after reading this and other books. There are still many "gray" areas for professionals on this subject, so don't feel frustrated if it does not seem perfectly clear to you. It's not always an easy call for us either.

A problem pronouncing words may be classified in a number of ways. Problems pronouncing words are called **articulation delays** (also called *articulation deficits* or *articulation disorders*). A child with an articulation delay may also have a **phonological disorder** or an **oral-motor weakness** (or *oral-motor deficit*), which are terms that describe the nature of the pronunciation problem. Frequently children have a combination of these problems. The degree and extent of the problem is characterized as *slight, mild, moderate,* or *severe.* By understanding the nature and degree of the pronunciation problem, the speech pathologist can better determine which therapy approach will be most effective. By understanding these differences, you can better understand why your child is having difficulty pronouncing words and why therapy often involves tasks other than practice saying words. Let's look at the three kinds of pronunciation problems: phonological disorders, simple articulation problems, and oral-motor weaknesses.

Phonological Disorders

Phonological disorders are speech problems that are more complex and pervasive than simple articulation deficits. When faced with a parent who is unfamiliar with this term, a speech pathologist sometimes may simply state that the child has a moderate or severe articulation problem. A child such as Ben, who is nearly impossible to understand, has a phonological problem.

Phonological disorders refer to the child's difficulty understanding the sound system itself and the speech rules that other children naturally pick up. A speech pathologist diagnoses a phonological disorder using standardized speech tests, as well as clinical observation.

A child with a phonological disorder may mispronounce a sound in certain words yet pronounce it clearly in other words. For example, the s in *sock* may be pronounced clearly, whereas the s in *bus* may not. Words that have two or more syllables may be pronounced with fewer syllables. For example, *elephant* may be pronounced as *ephant.*

Other times, whole groups of sounds are mispronounced the same way. For example, all s, f, sh, and ch sounds may be pronounced as a t. So a *sun* becomes a *tun*, a *chin* becomes a *tin*, a *fire* becomes a *tire*, and a *shoe* becomes a *too.* Children who mispronounce entire groups of sounds often need a special approach to learning to pronounce these sounds.

Sometimes a child with a phonological problem will leave out whatever sound is at the end of a word. For example, *book* is pronounced as *booh*, *juice* is pronounced as *joo,* and *bed* is pronounced as *beh.* The child may be able to easily pronounce the missing sounds when they occur in the beginning or middle of words yet leaves them off when they occur at the end of a word.

This can create special problems when the child pronounces words that have plural endings such as "toys" or "babies," possessive endings such as "Tommy's truck" or "Mommy's robe," or verb endings such as "walk*ed*" or "jump*ed.*" Those final sounds give the listener important information. In many cases, the child who leaves off these kinds of endings may also be described as having a *morphological deficit.* (This is described in greater detail in chapter 6.)

Therapy for a Child with a Phonological Disorder

The speech pathologist will help the child see that *ba* is a sound a sheep makes and that *bat* is different from *bath* and *back* and *bag*. By attaching different meanings to words by adding one little sound at the end of a word, a child will grow to understand the implications of leaving off that last sound. A child who leaves off the beginnings of words may benefit from a similar approach, with the emphasis placed on differentiating a word such as *at* from *bat, cat,* and *hat.* When a child leaves off the sounds at the end of a word, it also may signal a past or present hearing problem. Chapter 8 discusses speech problems of the hearing impaired in greater detail.

A child who has a phonological disorder is significantly at risk for developing problems when learning to read or spell and for other learning disabilities. Most of the same rules we learn for speaking must be understood for reading and writing. By improving the child's understanding of these rules, speech will improve, and so will the skills necessary for learning to read and write. Understanding these language rules is called metalinguistics. A child with a phonological problem will often benefit from learning these rules. Therapists teach metalinguistic rules by helping the child to understand the concept of rhyming, to identify words that start with a particular sound, to clap out syllables, and to distinguish between words of short and long length.

If your child is diagnosed with a phonological problem, you should be prepared for the possibility of a long-term commitment to speech therapy. You may find that considerable time will be spent on activities other than pronouncing words, which is often frustrating and confusing for parents. The long-term benefits for the child are substantial, however; in fact, many children speak "normally" in a few years.

Sometimes, correcting the speech problem also results in improved reading and spelling, but this is not always the case. The relationship between these areas is complex and still needs to be researched further.

In some cases, the child originally diagnosed as having a phonological disorder may later have difficulty pronouncing just one or two sounds. That child would then be described as having an articulation problem. For more on this, read on.

Simple Articulation Problems

When a child has a problem pronouncing a particular sound or a few sounds, it is called an articulation problem. Typically, such a child has consistent trouble saying that sound, or sounds, in every word in which the sound occurs. A number of factors may cause articulation problems, some of which are listed in chapter 8. In many cases, we don't know why a child has problems pronouncing certain sounds.

A child who is learning to speak the English language after living in another country or being raised by non-English-speaking parents will obviously have some pronunciation differences. This is called an *accent* and is not considered a speech disorder. Pronunciation of English will naturally improve in time if a child speaks English daily, is exposed to other children speaking English, and, yes, watches television. Most public schools do not have programs to change a child's accent. Adults may choose to work with a private speech pathologist, who can help with accent reduction.

As discussed in chapters 1 and 2, it is normal for infants and toddlers to have problems pronouncing words. But by the time children reach the end of second grade or so, most of the sounds should be pronounced clearly. Exactly when to recommend a child for speech therapy to "correct" a mispronounced sound is somewhat subjective and can depend on which developmental chart the speech pathologist is using. Many school systems have policies using the age of the child and severity of the problem as criteria to determine whether the child's speech is normal.

An articulation problem can be diagnosed using standardized tests that ask the child to name or describe certain pictures. But a speech pathologist can often diagnose simple problems by observing the child speaking in conversation. The speech pathologist looks at how the child pronounces words and examines the mouth to see whether a physical problem is interfering with the child's speech. Articulation may be just one of many areas examined when a child is experiencing other language or listening problems. As with phonological disorders, many children with articulation problems do, in fact, have other language and listening problems.

Children with hearing impairments, cleft palate, cerebral palsy, traumatic brain injury, and mental retardation tend to have unique articulation problems. These are discussed in chapter 8 in greater detail.

Therapy for a Child with an Articulation Problem

Therapy for articulation can often completely correct a child's mispronunciation of a particular sound within months. Some sounds (such as *r*), however, are a little more challenging and may take years to correct. Much of a child's success depends on the child's motivation, the parents' support, the amount of regular practice that takes place *at home*, physical conditions (such as cerebral palsy) that prohibit normal articulation, and the presence of other speech, language, and listening problems that may take precedence over an articulation problem. Following is some information about the most common articulation problems.

The *S* and *Z* Lisp

You have probably heard the term **lisp** before and have some idea of what it is. A lisp is regarded as a distortion of the *s* and *z* sounds. I lump these two sounds together because the problem affects them equally. They are produced in an identical manner, with the *z* being "voiced" by the vocal cords. To understand this better, make an *s* sound. While holding on to the *s* sound, try to make a *z* sound. The only thing you had to do was turn on your vocal cords. Your tongue never moved, and the air kept flowing, didn't it? Say the word *business*. The first *s* is produced more like a *z* than an *s*. The last *s* in the word is a true *s*. We produce *z* sounds more often than you think!

The *s* and *z* should be made by placing the tongue tip on the gum behind the top or bottom teeth and blowing out. To produce these sounds correctly, the tongue should not push on or between the teeth. If the tongue pushes forward, an *s* or *z* may sound more like a *th* sound, and the child is said to have a *frontal lisp* or *lingual protrusion*. If the *s* or *z* sounds "slushy," it is called a *lateral lisp*. Speech pathologists may refer to both of these types of lisps as *distortions*.

Is a lisp a problem? It depends on the child's age. Most children outgrow lisps by the age of 7 or 8. Speech problems that are typically outgrown are referred to as *developmental* speech problems.

Once your child is 7 or 8, other issues need to be considered:

- Does your child have a tongue thrust when swallowing? If so, you will probably need to address that as well as the lisp to make headway with the speech problem. If the tongue muscles are going the wrong way each time your child swallows, it will be difficult to retract the tongue properly when speaking. The speech pathologist or a dentist can tell you whether your child has a tongue thrust. (The problem of tongue thrust is discussed in greater detail later in this chapter.)
- Are you as a parent willing to devote the daily practice time required to successfully remediate this type of problem? Will your child be receptive to working on the activities? If the lisp does not bother your child or your child is resistant to the whole idea, speech therapy may be ineffective.
- Does your child's school provide therapy for lisps? If the lisp is

not adversely affecting your child's educational or emotional well-being, the public school may choose not to offer formal speech therapy. Private therapy may be quite costly.

Problems with *R* and *L*

Aside from the *s* and *z* sounds, the *r* and *l* sounds are probably the most commonly mispronounced. For these sounds, the tongue needs to pull up and slightly back. Doing this may be uncomfortable for the child if the tongue is somewhat restricted due to a shortened frenum. Though this is not a common problem, it does happen from time to time. In those cases, a dentist or speech pathologist may recommend that an oral surgeon evaluate the child for a procedure that can be performed under a local anesthesia to correct the problem.

Due to the nature of the *r* and *l,* sometimes it is necessary to wait until the muscles in the child's mouth are developmentally ready before beginning therapy. This usually happens by age 8 or so. Starting therapy too soon can prove frustrating for all involved, and by the time the child is physically ready to pronounce the sound, she may be turned off. This is a case where early intervention may not be the best idea.

Therapy for *r* and *l* may involve practicing exercises for the tongue and lip area before the sounds themselves are attempted. Likewise, it may help to develop the child's listening skills (**auditory discrimination**) before the child works on pronouncing the sounds, so that she can identify when the therapist says these sounds correctly or in which words.

Correcting *r* sounds in particular can sometimes require several years of therapy, and, occasionally, some children continue to have difficulty pronouncing the *r* despite diligent practice and effort.

Problems with *TH*

Many children have difficulty producing *th* sounds before they reach second grade or so. They typically produce these words with an *f* sound, which is a convenient and appropriate substitution because the two sounds are quite similar. If a child says, "I have a loose toof," everyone knows the word is *tooth.* This kind of speech problem really isn't a problem at all for a young child.

By the time a child reaches the age of 7 or 8, however, the *th* sound should be made correctly in conversational speech most of the time. If it isn't, and the child has no other speech problems, some home activities and short-term speech therapy should successfully correct the problem.

Oral-Motor Weaknesses

One of the most important parts of a speech evaluation is examining a child's **oral-motor skills.** If you think of the word *oral* as pertaining to the mouth area and *motor* as pertaining to how it moves, it will give you an idea as to what this means.

Children who have difficulty moving and controlling their mouths are sometimes called *apraxic.* Children with **apraxia** may be unable to open and close their mouth on demand, yet they can do so easily and naturally when yawning or biting into a sandwich. The difference is that they cannot do it when they want to. Children with apraxia sometimes have other neurological problems. They may also have difficulty moving other parts of their body when they want to. In toddlers, if apraxia is part of other maturational delays, it may be described as **developmental apraxia.**

Therapy for a Child with an Oral-Motor Weakness

Much of the early therapy for children with **oral-apraxia** may focus on gaining control of the mouth. For example, the speech pathologist will ask the child to perform certain tasks, such as sticking the tongue out, swallowing, chewing, opening and closing the mouth, and repeating certain syllables, such as *puh,* as quickly as possible.

In other children, the muscles used for speaking may be weak. For example, children may be able to control the movements of their tongue, lips, and cheeks but may not do so easily or with precision. For babies and preschoolers especially, the speech therapist may spend much time helping with eating and swallowing tasks to strengthen the associated muscles. Older children may spend time in front of a mirror lifting and holding their tongue in place or making funny faces. When a child drools or has difficulty chewing neatly or swallowing different textures of food, oral-motor weaknesses should be suspected. Children with "mumbly-sounding" speech often have oral-motor weaknesses.

A **tongue thrust** (also known as a *reverse swallow*) refers to the child's tongue thrusting forward between the teeth as swallowing takes place. This happens when the child is swallowing saliva or food. When a child with a tongue thrust eats, food can be pushed out slightly, which can look messy. In addition, you may notice the tongue sticking out, with the mouth slightly open, when the child is watching television, writing, or listening. Tongue thrusts, which are an imbalance of the tongue muscles, can cause or aggravate other speech or orthodontic problems. An oral-motor exam will clarify whether the child exhibits a tongue thrust. A speech pathologist or myofunctional therapist (or oro-facial myologist) has special training in this area and can prescribe exercises to correct the problem in a matter of months.

These are just a few of the typical oral-motor problems that may accompany or cause a speech problem. An oral-motor problem may be present at the same time a child exhibits an articulation or phonological disorder. If your child is diagnosed with oral-motor weaknesses, expect therapy to focus on nonspeech tasks such as lip exercises before, or along with, addressing the problem of pronouncing words.

Characteristics of Children with Pronunciation Problems

Children with pronunciation problems might do the following:

- Express frustration with the way they speak, particularly after the age of 2
- Need a parent or a sibling to interpret
- Be socially inhibited due to embarrassment about the speech problem
- Leave off the beginnings or endings of words
- Distort vowels
- Leave off entire syllables from longer words
- Not be understood much of the time by people outside the family, particularly after the age of 3
- Have speech that sounds unusual (not the typical lisp or "wabbit")

You probably don't need to worry if:

- Your child is understood most of the time (ages 3–6).
- Your child is understood all the time (ages 7 and up).

How Do Pronunication Problems Affect a Child?

For some children, a slight or mild speech problem such as a lisp has little or no direct effect on them at all. In fact, it is often more distracting or annoying to the person who is listening to them. Often these children have grown so accustomed to the way they speak that they are largely unaware that anything is unusual. Friends may have never mentioned, or ridiculed, the way the child speaks. Mild speech differences are easy to get used to, and rarely, if ever, cause any kind of learning difficulty in school. However, a tongue thrust left unchecked can lead to later orthodontic problems.

For children with moderate pronunciation problems, the effects are more clear. Studies have shown that adults and other children draw conclusions about a person by the way that person speaks. When a child has obvious pronunciation problems, others may assume the child is stupid. The older the child is, the more stigmatizing the speech problem is. Adolescents can be especially cruel and insensitive toward a peer and can seriously hurt that person's feelings.

When a child's speech is very difficult to understand, social development can sometimes be affected. Because the child has problems speaking clearly, others may need to have certain words repeated or explained if they are confused about what the child has said. After a while, the child may become frustrated and refuse to repeat the words, saying "Never mind, it wasn't important," rather than face the humiliation of mispronouncing the word yet again. Such a child may also participate very little in class discussions and become a passive observer in school. When a child feels uncomfortable participating in class, school can be a boring and awkward place.

As discussed earlier, some speech problems are associated with reading and spelling problems. A child who enters kindergarten with a moderate speech problem will be at a distinct disadvantage when trying to learn letters and sounds. For example, when asked to look at a picture of a kite and tell what the first sound or letter is, children will often write the sound they make when saying the word. So for a child who pronounces *kite* as *tite*, the answer is *t.*

Speech problems can also cause tension at home. Parents can sometimes be overzealous in trying to help children improve their speech. In their effort to remind a child to say words correctly, a parent can overdo it. Instead of being helped, the child may become resentful and resist speaking as the parent wishes. The child may also not be physically ready to incorporate the new skills into conversation and feel frustrated at letting the parent down. Communication with your child's therapist is important for this reason.

Some children resent the extra work at home that is essential to overcoming the speech problem and may resist at times. For a child with other learning or emotional problems, this added burden can indeed be troublesome and a source of conflict between parent and child.

A child with a severe speech problem who does not improve by first or second grade may also become quite self-conscious and experience lowered self-esteem and increased frustration. Feeling this way can certainly affect a child's behavior and even the way a child's personality develops. Some children react by being aggressive, rude, or temperamental; others become shy and say very little. Children with severe speech problems will need help coping and need to be motivated to keep working on improving their speech.

What Can Parents Do to Help a Child with a Pronunciation Problem?

If you have a child with a pronunciation problem, remember these points:

- Don't try to help by making the child repeat mispronounced words correctly, unless a professional suggests you do so. As discussed earlier in the chapter, there are sometimes complex reasons for your child's pronunciation problems. Perhaps your child's muscles are not ready to say those sounds, or maybe your child has not processed speech "rules" yet. You can make it worse by frustrating or embarrassing the child.
- If you can't understand your child, try to ask questions about what was said. Ask your child to say it again, but don't insist it be said your way. Sometimes I will say, "I'm sorry. I can't hear too well sometimes. Can you tell me that again?" Deep down, I think children know this game, but it takes the embarrassment off them and puts it on me. Parents have told me this works with them at home as well. With older children, it may suffice to say, "I'm sorry, I couldn't hear you. Could you repeat that?"
- Listen carefully to what your child says. Respond to the message and not the way it is said. *Never* say "You sound like a baby" (or "sissy," or any other negative label). Insulting your child into "speaking right" never works. Your child is not mispronouncing words on purpose. Young children, in particular, are not "lazy" talkers.
- Help your child's speech improve by following the speech pathologist's directions and performing any recommended activities as often as suggested. A few speech therapy sessions a week or less will have little impact and will take much longer to work if there is no consistent follow-through at home. I often tell parents that 90 percent of speech therapy should take place at home; the therapist merely introduces skills and strategies. Consider a child who takes a piano lesson every week yet never practices. That child will never master the piano. Similarly, the child who does

not practice speech exercises (recommended by a therapist) will not improve.

- Be patient. Improvement takes time. It may take years of hard work for a child to overcome a speech problem. Don't hound your child weeks or months after beginning therapy to start speaking correctly. Sometimes improvement comes in small steps. If you are feeling your child is not improving after a few months of therapy, talk to the therapist. Ask if the therapist has seen progress, and if so, in what way. Sometimes when you are so close to someone, you can miss those small, day-to-day changes. It may take an aunt who visits at the holidays to comment on the improvement in your child's speech for you to notice or believe it.

Case Study: Paul

Paul's mother called me when he was 4½. She was concerned about the way Paul was pronouncing words. She thought he would have "grown out of it" by now, but he hadn't. As I always do, I asked Paul's mother to bring him in to see me. As far as Paul knew, he was meeting a new "friend" at the school.

At this first meeting, the screening, Paul and I played with some plastic animals and puppets. We made them talk to each other. We looked at some picture books and made the characters pop up by pulling on a flap. We talked about those, too, and finished by playing with a plastic airport.

As a result of this visit, I could tell that Paul needed a more in-depth evaluation. His speech was very, very difficult to understand. He called an airplane a pay, *a tiger a* guh, *and a giraffe a* rah. *Many words were unidentifiable.*

I reviewed Paul's medical and birth history, and events such as when he began talking, with his mother. Nothing stood out about his birth or his early developing years. There was no history of frequent ear infections. All his other skills, such as walking, happened at the normal time. He was going to a preschool three days a week and interacted well with the other children. His mother also commented on how well Paul was doing with prekindergarten skills, such as counting and reciting the ABC's. In fact, he was already writing his name with little help.

With his mother's permission, I scheduled an evaluation to begin a week later. Paul had a good attention span during the testing, was cooperative, and answered all my questions thoughtfully. We took breaks so he wouldn't become too drained. I evaluated Paul's receptive language (what he understood) as well as expressive language (what he could say), in addition to his obvious pronunciation problems. The school nurse also checked his hearing and found it to be normal.

The results of the tests showed that Paul had severe articulation problems. He could be described as having a phonological disorder due to the nature of his mispronunciations. In addition, he had mild difficulty lifting his tongue up or back, so his oral-motor skills were also affected.

On the receptive language tasks, Paul showed a strong understanding of many language concepts such as behind and few. His understanding of vocabulary was also appropriate for his age. However, he did show some difficulty on the listening part of the test. Paul would easily forget directions if they were long, and he could not repeat a series of words back to me. If Paul had difficulty remembering what people said, it made sense that he would have difficulty remembering what the words were supposed to sound like when he tried to say them in conversation.

Paul began speech and auditory (listening) therapy soon thereafter. He came twice a week for a half hour. He and his parents worked diligently on the speech and listening activities sent home. Paul was sometimes resistant to practicing the activities, so we tailored a program based on football-oriented games, which was Paul's passion. For example, he practiced pronouncing the names of the players on his favorite team and used a paper football that he kicked with his finger to words on the "field."

By the time Paul finished kindergarten, he could be understood much of the time. As he felt more successful and confident, he was increasingly willing to try new, more difficult sounds. By the time he finished first grade, he was understood most of the time. His listening skills had also improved. By the time he finished third grade, he had difficulty pronouncing only r and l sounds and was reduced to one weekly therapy session. As a reward for using his corrected speech in conversation at home and in school, he was allowed to come once a month for "maintenance" in fourth grade. By the time he entered fifth grade, Paul spoke normally and was phased out of speech therapy.

Common Voice Problems

Johnnie has always sounded like he's getting over a case of laryngitis. I figured it was just the way he talked, so it never seemed like a "problem" to me. He coughs a lot from allergies, so I'm sure that's not helping. Some days he's "squeakier" than others, but nobody has

trouble understanding what he says. He's always yelling over his three brothers, I'll tell you that! I don't have any reason to worry, do I?
—Mother of Johnnie, age 6

Maybe, maybe not. Although Johnnie is usually understood easily, he is straining every time he talks. A number of things can happen when putting constant stress on the vocal cords. Some are serious; others are simply annoying.

Speaking requires the cooperation of several body parts. Your vocal cords alone do not dictate how your voice sounds. Your lungs and chest muscles are a very important part of the speaking process. Nerves in the brain control the vocal cords and their ability to work properly. The tissue in the back of your throat and in your nose help give your voice its unique sound quality. So, when we talk about the "voice," remember that many parts of the body play a part in how the voice sounds.

The voice is a highly sensitive instrument and is our own personal "signature." The way we sound when we speak can say a lot about us. Think of famous actors and actresses such as Jimmy Stewart, John Wayne, Jack Nicholson, Billy Crystal, Kathleen Turner, and Gracie Allen. Their voices set the tone for the types of characters they played and helped establish a certain image.

Fortunately, Johnnie doesn't have to worry about an image. He's only 6 years old. But he does have one of the more common types of voice problems that we'll discuss in this section. (Voice problems related to cerebral palsy, Down syndrome, hearing impairment, cleft palate, and traumatic brain injury are discussed in chapter 8.)

Diagnosis and Causes of Voice Problems

In a common case of laryngitis, some vocal strain is expected and should be gone in a week or two. However, when your child's voice sounds "froggy," "squeaky," or "hoarse" on a regular basis or for weeks or months at a time, it should be checked out. You may ask a speech pathologist to listen to your child speak if you are not sure there is truly enough hoarseness for you to be concerned. However, no speech pathologist will or should attempt any kind of therapy or intervention until a medical doctor has examined the child and given the green light to do so.

The doctor who examines the vocal cords is called an *otolaryngologist,* also known as an ear, nose, and throat doctor. The doctor needs to see the vocal cords to find out what is causing the hoarseness. The vocal cords may be examined with fiberoptics, which are wire-thin tubes that are typically fed through the nose to the vocal cord area. This allows the doctor to watch the vocal cords, move as the child is asked to make certain sounds. It is a slightly uncomfortable procedure, but not painful. A local anesthetic can be sprayed to make it more comfortable. Another way of examining the vocal cords, called *laryngoscopy,* uses strategically placed mirrors in the back of the mouth. Sometimes children gag when this technique is used, so it may be difficult to see the vocal cords clearly or for an extended period of time. New technology for examining the **larynx** emerges almost daily.

So what should the doctor see? The vocal cords are shaped like a small V in the middle. They sit in the windpipe (pharynx). The air you breathe goes through the opening in the V. The inside edges have very thin membranes that need to touch back and forth without interference in order to produce sound. When you speak, they vibrate many times as the air passes through from the lungs. When one side has a growth or is thicker than the other, the vocal cords (*vocal folds*) will not be synchronized properly when they vibrate. This results in a gravelly sounding, or hoarse, voice.

Both physical and medical conditions can cause a child's voice to sound hoarse or strained. The most common causes are vocal polyps or vocal nodules. which can be a result of the child using the vocal cords incorrectly.

Vocal Polyps

Vocal polyps are fluid-filled sacs that can form on the lining of the vocal cords. Usually only one side of the vocal cords has a polyp. It can be caused initially by straining the voice on just one occasion, such as singing during a long, loud concert. If the child continues to overuse his voice, the strained cord is further irritated and the polyp will grow. A child with a polyp may sound breathy or hoarse and may feel like clearing his throat because it feels like something is "down there." Unfortunately, clearing the throat can make the problem worse, because it irritates the polyp.

Vocal Nodules

Vocal nodules are small callous growths that can start on one side of the vocal cords. As the irritated side bangs against the other vocal cord when vibrating, its hardness irritates the other side of the vocal cords. So it is fairly common to see two vocal nodules, one on each side, in a child with a long-term hoarseness problem. Nodules are typically caused by a long-term source of irritation, such as cheerleading, yelling, or speaking loudly too often, chronic coughing, or singing or speaking with stress or strain (another example of vocal abuse). Nodules are more common in boys and more common than vocal polyps. The child with vocal nodules will tend to get "tired of talking" and become more hoarse as the day wears on. It may be difficult for the child to speak loudly or yell without discomfort.

If a vocal polyp or nodule is left untreated, the child may continue to work even harder to speak, causing the problem to become more and more noticeable until he can hardly speak above a throaty whisper. If you wait too long, surgery may sometimes become the only option.

Papilloma

Papilloma is a wartlike growth that can occur in the vocal cord area of children. The majority of papilloma cases occur in children under the age of 6. When speaking, the child may sound as though she has vocal polyps or vocal nodules. The papilloma can eventually block the child's airway, causing difficulty breathing. This, along with other less common medical problems, is one of the most important reasons why hoarseness in a child should not be taken lightly and should be assessed by a physician. The treatment for papilloma is strictly medical. It is not caused or aggravated by how a child speaks. Surgery involving lasers, followed by voice rest, may be necessary to remove the papilloma.

Other medical problems can also cause a hoarse voice. Hemangiomas, granulomas, and laryngeal "webbing" are not common but do occur. Intubation during a surgical procedure or a blow to the windpipe, as well as infection or disease, can set these in motion. These problems are not caused by misuse of the voice, and they require medical attention. Again, simply listening to a voice is not enough to make an accurate diagnosis. A medical examination that looks directly at the vocal cords is necessary to rule out these problems.

Many times children with hoarse or breathy voices do not exhibit any medical problem with their vocal cords during an exam. It is usually advisable in this case to help the child change the **vocal abuse** pattern (speaking or using the voice in an unhealthy way) that is causing the hoarseness, because continued strain can eventually (but does not always) lead to growths, such as nodules, and then, sometimes, surgery. Young boys and teenage girls are high-risk groups for vocal abuse behavior. In addition, children who are "high-strung" may put undue stress on their voices.

Characteristics of Children with Voice Problems

Children with voice problems might do the following:

- Make "squeaking" sounds when speaking
- Run out of air before finishing a normal sentence
- Not speak loudly enough to be heard across a room
- Sound hoarse, harsh, "husky," or "gravelly" for more than ten days or have frequent bouts of "laryngitis" throughout a single year
- Clear their throats frequently
- Sound more "throaty" by the end of the day than in the morning
- Open their mouths and have nothing come out for a second or so
- Sound like two people are talking at the same time, but with different pitches
- Have their voice crack while talking
- Sound strained and "throaty" when laughing or crying

How Do Voice Problems Affect a Child?

Vocal hoarseness may not cause much of a problem for some children, especially in the early stages. Aside from medically related problems, vocal hoarseness may be more of a nuisance than anything else. The problem, of course, is the long-term effect on the strength and quality of the child's voice, and the possibility of surgery if the hoarseness gets worse. I have known children who have gone through 12 years of school with a mildly hoarse voice, which, for the most part, has gotten neither worse nor better. For them and their parents, it wasn't a problem worth fretting about. This is especially true when a child, like Johnnie, has always talked this way.

For other children, however, vocal hoarseness has more serious effects. In addition to the possible long-term effects previously mentioned, if left untreated, vocal hoarseness can seriously impact some children's ability to communicate and participate effectively in class. For this reason, voice therapy should be offered in most schools in the United States. Whether a child's voice problem affects academic performance is the criterion typically used to determine whether a child qualifies for public school speech therapy, but there is some subjectivity in determining this relationship. Don't forget that you as a parent have the right to a hearing if you are not satisfied with the results of your school's recommendation. Hospitals and private practices often offer advantages of high-tech equipment that can give your child feedback when speaking and chart progress using instruments that measure certain characteristics of the voice. Computer programs that offer similar features can often be found in a school as well.

Therapy for a Child with a Voice Problem

When a vocal polyp or nodule is found, the doctor may ask a speech therapist to try some therapy and behavior changes for a few months to see whether the growth decreases. If it does not, surgery may be necessary to remove the growth, followed by voice rest, which means total silence (not even whispering) for a week or more. After the vocal cord has healed, speech therapy will again be important, because the problem will recur if the child continues the old vocal abuse pattern.

Correcting the problem with speech therapy rather than surgery alone is important. Repeated surgeries take a toll on the vocal cords, because a layer of membrane is literally stripped away. Scar tissue from repeated surgeries may cause further irritation, making more surgery ineffective. By changing the way the child speaks, the vicious circle can be broken.

Treating voice problems caused by vocal abuse focuses on changing the behaviors that strain the vocal cords. A child like Johnnie, with allergies, should have them treated promptly. Every time Johnnie coughs, clears his throat, or sneezes, he is causing his vocal cords to slam together in a very stressful way. If he likes to make loud car noises with his throat or grunt when playing with toy action figures, his condition will worsen. His mother may need to organize "quiet talking time" in the house so he doesn't need to shout over siblings to be heard.

If changes in the child's routine don't improve the voice enough, speech or "voice" therapy may be helpful. The therapy will help the child speak in a manner that is less stressful on the voice.

Changing or controlling the way a young child uses his or her voice is, however, no easy task. Boys in particular like to make a variety of noises when playing and are significantly more prone to vocal abuse. Imitating car engines, crashing planes, horns or sirens, animal noises, and those "AAHHHHH!" sounds as a child jumps into a pool, rides the roller coaster, or plays cops and robbers are all a normal way of playing for many children. But for some, such noisy play can aggravate a voice problem.

Many times children resent having to curtail or monitor the sounds they make. For young children, thinking consciously about what they say or do is very difficult, if not impossible. All the reminders and rewards in the world may be fruitless. Parents tell me they feel guilty if they don't stop their child each time this happens. Yet when they do, they feel like the bad guy, who is trying to take away their child's fun. There are no easy answers, and sometimes the problem may have to linger and be medically monitored until the child is old enough to understand what to do.

What Can Parents Do to Help a Child with a Voice Problem?

If your child demonstrates any of the characteristic behaviors of a voice problem for more than a few weeks, have a doctor check it out. An ear, nose, and throat doctor is preferable, but a general practitioner or pediatrician may suffice if you don't have access to a specialist. The most important step you can take is to ensure there is not a serious medical problem causing the voice change. If the doctor feels it is appropriate, a referral to a speech therapist may be made. Once a diagnosis has been made, keep these thoughts in mind:

- Try to help your child change speaking habits by following the speech therapist's recommendations carefully.
- Keep a quiet home. Make sure your child doesn't have to be heard over loud music or noisy dishwashers.
- If voice rest is recommended, it is imperative that your child make no sound at all in order for this treatment to have the desired effect. This means no laughing, crying, or whispering, although this is often difficult to control in a child.
- Make sure all allergies, respiratory, and sinus problems are addressed so that your child does not have to cough, sneeze, or clear the throat frequently.
- Keep the radio off in the car so that your child doesn't have to shout over it to be heard.
- Help your child get in the habit of walking over to the person she wants to speak to, instead of yelling across the room or down the stairs.
- Though voice problems usually do not result in the academic problems or social awkwardness that other speech problems

sometimes do, monitor the condition of your child's voice carefully to prevent future relapses.

Case Study: Frank

Frank's mother called me after a visit to her son's ear, nose, and throat doctor. Frank, a bright and active 8-year-old, had been to the doctor for an examination of his ears, which seemed to have yet another infection. While there the doctor noticed Frank's unusually raspy-sounding voice. His mother commented that his voice had been gradually getting more and more hoarse over the past six months. It was so gradual that she hardly noticed it until the doctor mentioned it.

As the doctor examined Frank's vocal cords and asked him to imitate certain sounds, he noticed the beginning of a vocal nodule on Frank's left vocal cord. He suggested Frank receive speech therapy to prevent any further growth or resulting irritation on the right vocal cord. If the therapy was successful, the present growth might subside completely.

When I met with Frank's mother, we discussed his speaking habits as well as other behaviors that might aggravate the vocal nodule. She reported he had a postnasal drip from his allergies, which caused him to cough and clear his throat frequently. We discussed why it would be helpful to have this medically managed so that Frank didn't need to strain his voice. Because Frank was having problems hearing, he was speaking more loudly than a typical child. His doctor found residual fluid lingering in Frank's middle ear as a result of frequent ear infections. When antiobiotics and antihistamines were unsuccessful in eliminating the fluid, tubes were inserted, which immediately improved Frank's hearing to within normal limits. As a result, his voice volume returned to a more normal level.

At Frank's house, his teenage brother apparently liked to blast the stereo. Thus, Frank often yelled up the basement steps from the playroom to his mother in the kitchen to be heard over the din of the stereo. We discussed how he would need to walk up the steps instead of yelling, and how the stereo would have to be turned down when Frank wanted to talk. Frank also had a habit of making a loud grunting noise whenever he threw a basketball toward the hoop on his driveway. Since he played basketball every afternoon, that was a lot of grunting!

We agreed to work on these and other changes to help improve Frank's voice habits. We then discussed these changes, and the reasons for them, with Frank. I saw Frank every week for six weeks after this meeting to discuss his week and monitor his progress. I began to notice some improvement in his voice quality. Unfortunately, because voice cases are not widespread, my school (like most) did not have sophisticated instru-

ments, as some hospitals do, to objectively measure the changes in Frank's voice. However, a good ear and careful notes sufficed.

By the end of three months, Frank's voice sounded relatively normal. I asked his mother to have his doctor reexamine him. We were pleased to learn that all evidence of the vocal nodule was gone. We never did need to initiate formal voice therapy with Frank. The problem was caught fairly early and responded well to some behavior changes.

Frank's mother tells me that he occasionally slips back into his old habits and does need some reminding. If she notices the hoarseness returning, she immediately helps Frank work extra hard to be "nice" to his voice. He has never had his vocal nodule return.

6

Understanding
Language Problems

"Your child has an expressive language delay." Just what does this mean?
Language is a very broad term. As we discussed in chapter 1, language
is divided into receptive and expressive components. If your child is
diagnosed with an expressive language delay, you will want to find out
exactly what *kind* of expressive (or receptive) language weakness your
child is exhibiting.

In this chapter, I describe the symptoms and typical intervention of
the most common language problems. I also explain how a child is affected by each problem and what you as a parent can do to help. Some
of the early language problems of infants, toddlers, and preschoolers
discussed in this chapter include developmental delays (sometimes
called "maturational" problems), sensory integration deficits, and fluctuating hearing loss.

As children get older, they may have trouble understanding words
(receptive vocabulary problems) and/or using words (expressive vocabulary problems). They may also have difficulty with morphology (word
forms), syntax (grammar), word retrieval, and using language to express
what they mean. All of these problems are covered in this chapter.

A speech-language pathologist examines many aspects of a child's
use of language to see if he or she is developing language normally. Some
of the activities that are analyzed include the following:

- Speaking and communicating in social settings (pragmatics)
- Putting a sentence together (syntax)

- Using words (semantics)
- Retelling the plot to a story (sequencing)
- Changing word endings, depending on the context (morphology)
- Learning word meanings (vocabulary)
- Remembering words learned before (word retrieval)

Some children have a weakness in only one particular area. But for most children with expressive language problems, several of these language areas are affected at one time.

Language problems are not something you can easily "cure." Just as some children will never be adept at math or the long jump, some children will always be weak conversationalists. Learn to accept your child as a unique individual and emphasize the things he or she does well. Try not to make the language problem bigger than it is. Yes, it is a shame to be burdened with these difficulties, but with the right help language problems need not be an obstacle to a successful and happy life.

Infants, Toddlers, and Preschoolers with Delayed Speech and Language

Jessica is a very bright child, so I know there can't be anything wrong with her. Besides, we've given her so much stimulation from the time she was in the womb! Still, my sister keeps telling me that maybe she should be saying more than a few words at 2½ years old. My pediatrician doesn't seem concerned, so I guess I'll just wait a few years and see if she outgrows it.

—Mother of Jessica, age 2½

Just because Jessica is having a "slow start" with her speech and language development, it does not necessarily mean she is mentally "slow" or will struggle with a lifelong problem. That is why, in most cases, difficulties at this age are called *delays* as opposed to *disorders*. It doesn't mean her mother and father haven't done a wonderful job stimulating her. And, although pediatricians can be quite helpful, they are not trained speech therapists. So if you are concerned about your child's language development, consult the specialist trained in this area, a speech-language pathologist.

Chapters 1 and 2 showed you that a child exhibiting Jessica's speech pattern is not progressing as expected. In this section, you'll discover what kind of problem a child like Jessica may be having and what her parents can do to help her.

Although nature has a hand in how a child develops, don't underestimate the power of a nurturing parent. In this section, you will also learn just how significant that role is and how you can make the most of the time you have with your child at this important age.

Children under the age of five have special considerations when it comes to speech and language development. Because there is a wide range of what is considered normal language development at this time, many delays are just that, delays. At times, however, a child's language development needs special attention.

Delays in Speech or Language Only

Jessica, described at the beginning of this section, seemed to be developing normally in every way except for her speech. Sometimes this happens. In many cases, we really don't know why. A *developmental delay* (also called a *maturational* problem) simply means the child is not developing in one area as expected. It is a descriptive term, making no judgment as to whether the problem is permanent. In a case such as Jessica's, her parents should seek an evaluation. The speech-language pathologist may choose to make home visits because of Jessica's young age and work with Jessica's parents to help stimulate her interest in talking and communicating, using informal activities. Activities to develop her listening skills will also be included if needed.

In most cases, after about six months, the therapist will evaluate how the child is progressing. Sometimes children like Jessica make rapid progress and will need to come in only for periodic check-ups to monitor their speech and language development. If progress is slower than expected, a more aggressive approach should be considered. Formal speech-language therapy sessions may be scheduled, often at a public school site. Therapy sessions are play oriented and are usually fun for the child.

In many cases, a child like Jessica may be speaking and comprehending normally (or near normally) by the time kindergarten comes and may experience no difficulty in school. In more involved cases, the child will continue to need help. When a child has a significant delay in speaking or listening, there is some risk that academic problems may surface later, even if the speech or language problem itself is corrected (Gerber & Bryen, 1981; Lewis & Freebairn, 1992). However, mild pronunciation problems are not usually a sign of later difficulties.

The research does not yet tell us which children will have problems later. However, if a child begins school already identified as having a speech or language delay, the staff will monitor progress closely and implement special teaching strategies if academic problems start to develop.

Pervasive Developmental Delay

When young children are identified as having significant delays in several skill areas (such as learning basic concepts, playing with peers, balance, and attention span), it is often called **Pervasive Developmental Delay (PDD).** Children with PDD typically have significant difficulty understanding and using language in a normal way. The nature of PDD is often elusive. Some children catch up, and some don't. Unfortunately, knowing who will and who won't is not an exact science. Much research still needs to be done to answer these questions. For this reason, diagnosing and prognosing before the age of 7 is tricky and should be done with extreme caution. Is the child a "late bloomer," or is this the beginning of a long-term handicapping condition? Typically, by age 7 or so, a child's neurological system has matured enough to determine whether the problems are serious or long term.

Although you will be understandably anxious to know what lies ahead for your child if she is diagnosed with PDD, you must guard against either false hopes that can set you up for disappointment or lowered expectations that can become a self-fulfilling prophecy. Many educators and specialists refer to these children as being "pervasive developmentally delayed" rather than "learning-disabled," "autistic," or "slow," because PDD is a bit of a catchall; that is, it describes the symptoms, not necessarily the cause or prognosis. Children with this classification may (but will not necessarily) later be assigned a more specific diagnosis and label.

Only time will tell if a child with pervasive developmental delays will catch up. An appropriate educational program, often combined with a traditional preschool placement, increases the chances for the child to reach full potential. In the United States, a team of specialists called a multidisciplinary team, staffed or contracted by your local school system, helps design the program and establish therapeutic goals. Usually a physical therapist, occupational therapist, special education teacher, psychologist, and speech pathologist make up this team. (Chapter 3 gave more information on how to go about setting up this kind of evaluation.)

Sensory Integration Problems

Another cause of speech, language, and listening delays in young children is an overloading or confusion of messages received by their bodies.

An infant learns about the world by tasting, touching, smelling, hearing, and seeing. When the brain fails to process these sensations correctly, the child is often unable to make sense of the world. Listening and speaking delays are just two symptoms of a *sensory integration problem.*

Noisy places, such as malls and parties, normally overstimulate infants because the sights and sounds overwhelm them. This often results in crankiness or screaming (which are ways of expressing discomfort) or sleepiness (which is a way of withdrawing). As infants grow into 3- or 4-year-olds, their neurological systems are better able to process these sights and sounds. For children with sensory integration problems, however, the sights, sounds, and commotion are too much to handle at once, even at 3 or 4 years of age. Crying outbursts or withdrawal are typical ways these children cope when their circuits overload. In fact, many people now believe autistic children have a more severe form of sensory integration dysfunction.

Often the child with a sensory integration weakness displays difficulties in other areas, particularly with physical coordination and/or balance, as well as attention span. In this case, you should consult a physical therapist or occupational therapist specially trained in sensory integration. In rural areas, this may be easier said than done. Some schools contract with occupational and physical therapists who come in to provide services to students who need it. These specialists should be utilized to assist in a thorough evaluation and treatment plan.

To address the communication needs of children with sensory integration problems, a speech-language pathologist should work closely with the child and any other professionals involved. This intervention may be in the form of formal therapy sessions or as part of a team within a special preschool classroom. Often these children respond best when speech and language therapy is integrated into a more natural setting, such as the home or school environment.

Many sensory integration deficits improve significantly with appropriate therapeutic intervention and time. As the children mature, it may be difficult for an untrained eye to notice any problem at all. In other cases, the problems persist. Children with severe, persistent sensory integration problems may later be diagnosed as autistic or learning-disabled.

Congenital Conditions

Babies born with diagnosed conditions such as Down syndrome, Hunter's syndrome, cerebral palsy, deafness, or cleft palate typically have speech, language, or listening problems. In most cases, doctors can diagnose congenital problems at birth. In some cases, however, particularly with deafness, a problem does not become apparent until the child does not develop in some way as expected. Congenital problems are usually diagnosed in the first year or two by your child's pediatrician.

A child with a congenital problem will need more stimulation than the typical child and will often need a specialized educational program. Hospitals assist with setting up these programs at birth. Insurance companies sometimes cover the cost of speech or physical therapy services. U.S. public schools are now being asked to provide services from birth for children with handicapping conditions, typically through a regional agency. (In Canada, all speech therapy for infants is handled through the Health Ministry.)

In many cases, speech-language therapy is provided directly in the home until a child is 3 years old. The typical focus of therapy is to develop muscles in the mouth used for feeding, as well as speaking. Also, parents and caregivers are instructed in ways to facilitate the child's speech and language skills in daily situations.

As the child approaches the 3-year mark, therapy may take the form of a preschool program run by the local school system. In this kind of program, therapists work with the preschool teacher to plan activities that help the child develop needed skills. In recent years, many programs combine children with special needs with a typical preschool population. As mentioned previously, this allows the children with special needs to imitate the speech and behavior of peers who can set a good example. Typical children also benefit from the program because the program is free, has a low teacher-pupil ratio, and allows the children to get used to learning side by side with children with learning differences. In Canada, the way services are delivered varies from province to province and from school to school.

For children with signficant speech and language delays, particularly with deafness and cleft palate, aggressive speech-language therapy is usually necessary.

Fluctuating Hearing Loss from Middle Ear Fluid

When children have delays in speech, language, or listening skills, the problem could be caused by fluid in the middle ear left over from a cold, allergies, or ear infection. Often the only symptoms that the child with fluctuating hearing loss displays are crankiness or tugging on the ear. Due to the physical structure of a young child's ear and eustachian tube, middle ear fluid problems are prevalent in children under the age of 7.

The fluid cannot always be detected by simply looking into the ear with an otoscope. A machine called a **tympanometer** can detect middle ear fluid. A rubber-tipped probe is inserted into the child's outer ear, which is usually only slightly uncomfortable for the child, if not painless. It sends sound waves through the ear canal and measures how they travel. An audiologist, nurse, or physician can perform this test. Children with chronic middle ear fluid might display the following symptoms:

- Begin talking late or even go "backward," that is, talk less than a few months ago
- Not turn around or respond when you call their name. This is particularly true if the TV is on or you are in a noisy environment.
- Speak with an overall "mumbly" quality
- Say "what?" or "huh?" often
- Leaves off endings frequently. For example, the child may say, "I saw fie (five) cat on the gra (grass). One hop up and down!"
- Breathe through the mouth because the nose is too congested
- Have a short attention span for conversation or stories unless there are pictures to look at

Fluctuating hearing loss is often caused by ear infections. If your child has frequent ear infections, treating the infection with antibiotics alone may not always do the trick. Although the fever may subside, the fluid can linger unnoticed and produce no outward symptoms. Since your child is in no apparent discomfort, it would seem that the infection and its effects have passed. But though the leftover fluid may not be a health concern, it does present another threat. There is research linking frequent early middle ear infections to later problems in school (Hasenstab, 1987; Roberts, Burchinal, Davis, Collier, & Henderson, 1991).

In the past, many doctors thought they were doing a child a favor by resisting the insertion of ventilation tubes in the child's ears when fluid is persistent. After all, why subject a child to surgery unless it is absolutely necessary? However, in 1994, the Agency for Health Care Policy and Research (AHCPR) of the U.S. Public Health Service announced treatment guidelines for children with chronic middle ear fluid. Ventilation tubes are now recommended as a standard procedure if the fluid has not subsided in four to six months, after observation or antibiotics has proven ineffective. Although the tubes may not be an absolute medical necessity, they do allow a child to hear speech and language more *clearly*. By hearing verbal information more clearly, your child can discriminate sounds, tell words apart, and imitate the words you say more correctly.

Therapeutic intervention for these children depends on how delayed the child is and whether there has been spontaneous improvement once the fluid is gone. In many cases, if caught early, therapy is needed only on a short-term basis if at all. Frequently, the parent can do some activities at home to stimulate speech and language as suggested by the speech pathologist to meet the child's individual needs. In other cases, a child may need long-term therapy and academic assistance.

Characteristics of Young Children with Speech or Language Delays

Any child exhibiting the characteristics of a speech, language, or listening disorder should have a hearing screening. Chapter 2 details the warning signs for children with speech and language delays. Children under age 3 who have delayed speech or language might do the following:

- Chew and swallow food with difficulty or reject food that is difficult to chew
- Drink or suck through a straw with difficulty
- Sit with their mouth open and tongue forward
- Choke on drinks and food more often than other children do
- Have trouble sensing when food is left on the face after eating
- Show little interest in imitating words and sounds
- Avoid eye contact with parents and other familiar people
- Use gestures or noises to indicate wants
- Have little interest in listening to stories or looking at books with a parent
- Be very quiet and passive; seldom initiate interaction
- Not respond to or imitate common baby games, such as waving bye-bye or playing peek-a-boo
- Not use recognizable words with consistency (after about 14 months of age)
- Not make noise or experiment with their voices in playful ways

The characteristics for children between the ages 3 and 5 also vary because children change so quickly at these ages. Chapter 2 describes speech and language symptoms that signal a need for further evaluation. Children between 3 and 5 who have delayed speech or language might do the following:

- Appear very frustrated when people don't understand what they want

- Dislike and/or avoid reciting nursery rhymes
- Sing songs with poor recall of the words, even when heard on a daily basis
- Still eat with some difficulty; need to have food chopped up more than other children of the same age
- Drink thick liquids through a straw (such as a milkshake) with difficulty
- Rely on gestures to supplement what they say
- Use puppets or dolls but with little talking
- Have difficulty explaining events that have caused them to be upset; the parent needs to ask an inordinate number of questions to understand what happened
- Watch a movie or TV show but be unable to tell important parts of the story afterward
- Listen to a familiar story, heard frequently, but be unable to flip the pages and retell the story

How Do Early Language Delays Affect a Child?

Children who have difficulty communicating have even more opportunities for temper tantrums than do typical children. For example, if a child like Jessica wants a glass of a particular kind of juice, she may grab her mother's hand, bring her to the refrigerator, and point to what she wants. If there are many things in the refrigerator, her mother may have to ask her a number of questions before she picks up the item Jessica wants. "Do you want some milk?" Jessica's response to this question is most likely a shake of her head to indicate no. "Do you want some grapes?" At this point, Jessica's response is likely to be a whiny cry. Because she is only 2½, Jessica doesn't understand why her mother cannot literally read her mind. When her mother does not pick up the juice she wants, her reaction is frustration. Most children under the age of 5 or so display frustration by crying, stamping feet, whining, or falling to the floor. And in many cases, unfortunately, a child exhibits all of these behaviors. The good news is that, in my experience, the frequency of these kinds of behaviors is reduced dramatically once a child is able to communicate more successfully.

Other children, particularly those with accompanying brain damage, may cope with their language delays by being passive. They sit patiently and wait for others to initiate interaction. Because they are unable to communicate their feelings, they may give up trying and sometimes retreat into their own little world. These children can sit in front of a TV for hours at a time and never fuss. Although these passive children are easier to manage behaviorally, as a therapist, I am more hopeful when parents tell me how frustrated and whiny their language-delayed child is. Even though it is more taxing for you, it is an important sign that your child *wants* to communicate, which is the first critical step toward learning to speak.

It is hard to determine how early language delays affect children socially. Because they can't tell us how they feel, we have to draw conclusions from what we see. Some language-delayed children do become shy and uneasy with other children; others are undaunted and will tumble, run, and play blocks with the gang as any other child would. Several factors seem to affect how a language-delayed child interacts with other children.

- *Does the child have any other handicapping condition?* For example, if the child is having trouble hearing or walking, many activities may be more difficult to join in. For these children, creative play solutions with your child's therapist may be in order.
- *Does the child have a naturally shy personality?* For this child, the added burden of a language delay will certainly make playing with other children more challenging.
- *Does the child have opportunities to meet other children?* For a language-delayed child, physical activities such as tumbling, karate, or arts and crafts can provide a nonthreatening social environment where what they can do is more important than what they can say.

As for the future, a child with an early language delay may eventually catch up and have no further learning problems, if there are no other areas of delay. Even a child with no other delays, however, is at risk for *possibly* developing learning disabilities later on if language development is slow. If a specific problem accompanies the language delay, such as neurological impairment, retardation, hearing impairment, or autism, the prognosis is difficult to generalize because each child's progress is unique.

What Can Parents Do to Help Develop Early Language Skills?

Parents often ask me what they can do to help develop their child's speech, language, and listening skills. In some cases, parents want to help a child with delayed speech or listening skills catch up; other parents want to maximize a child's potential by building a solid foundation before anything goes wrong. The following are some keys to help your child achieve his or her potential:

- *Listen to your child with enthusiasm and interest.* If you want your child to talk, you must show interest in what the child is saying. Stop what you are doing and look at your child as you look at an adult when listening. Children *do* know when you are half-listening as you watch TV or read the newspaper. Though the bug outside may not be so exciting to you, your 3-year-old is eager to share the news with you. Try your best to respond with some enthusiasm and interest, no matter how mundane a child's discovery seems to you. Ask questions about it. Share information about the subject the child is talking about. Children who feel that what they say is of no importance are less likely to keep trying to communicate in a desirable way. In other words, they may try to get your attention with aggressive or whiny behavior instead.

- *Read to your child every day.* I can't overstate the importance of reading to your child. Simple books (usually cardboard and with few pages) that are designed to teach word names right from birth are available. Establish a routine and comfort with books. It also is a nice way to have private mother-child or father-child time. Go to the library every week, and as children reach the age of 2 or 3, let them pick out books that interest them. Read your child's favorite books over and over, ten times a day if your child wants! Talk about the stories and the picture names. Let your child "read" them to you. If he wants to change the story, let him be creative. Show interest in his ideas. If the story your child selects is too long or wordy, shorten and simplify it as you go along. Young children have a very short attention span, so you may not want to spend too long on one page. As your child gets older, you can incorporate more and more of the actual words on the page.

- *Resist talking like your child or encouraging baby talk.* Some parents imitate a child's infantile way of saying a word, thinking it is cute or helpful to the child. For example, if Arden calls a blanket a "boo-boo," Mom may get in the habit of asking Arden to get his "boo-boo." If only a few words are involved, that's fine. Just don't overdo it! However, if Mom or Dad begin incorporating baby talk more and more into their own vocabulary, the child may lose the incentive and opportunity to learn the correct way of saying words. By imitating your child's pronunciation, you are giving him the impression that this is the right way to say it. By talking like an adult, you afford your child the opportunity to hear and attempt the correct way to speak.

• *Avoid letting older siblings speak for your child.* Sometimes we observe children whose older siblings try to help by speaking for their younger brother or sister when the younger one is asked a question. Unfortunately, their dominance can often lead a younger child to be less verbal and less comfortable in initiating conversations. If you find an older sibling doing the talking for a younger child, encourage the child to speak for herself.

• *Praise any attempt at speaking—perfection is not the goal.* Some parents, in their zeal to foster good speaking skills, push for perfection when their child is learning to talk. This kind of pressure is not helpful. Your child can read criticism in your tone of voice, facial expression, or persistent request to "say it again the right way." A child picks up on this disapproval and may react by feeling inhibited and less willing to attempt to speak. Learning to speak requires practice, practice, and more practice! If a child feels comfortable in failing, she will be more apt to try again, probably in another situation and time, without being forced.

You can help in this regard by showing enthusiasm for *any* attempt at speaking and putting words together. A smile and repetition of what the child said (in corrected form) shows the child you understand *and* approve of what was said. The conversation below is an example of a positive exchange between a parent and child.

Mom: What would you like for lunch, Jessie?
Jessie: How 'bou andith (sandwich)?
Mom: A sandwich? Okay, what kind of sandwich?
Jessie: Peanut buttoo and delly.
Mom: I think we have peanut butter and jelly.

• *Talk with your child about everything—being together is not enough.* Some parents, when reviewing test results with me, will show surprise when I tell them their child was unable to name a goat, a necklace, or other object. Consider 5-year-old Gina's mother and father, for instance. "Gee," her mother said, "little Gina sees those all the time. We're so careful about bringing her to see things, like the animals on the farm. How can she not know their names?"·

On further discussion, Gina's parents reconstructed the visits to the farm and museum and realized that the visit was accompanied by some of Gina's cousins, Aunt Amy Jo, and Uncle Ben. Who were Mom and

Dad talking to during this visit? Actually, the adults talked about business, the weather, politics, you name it. The children ran around and fed some of the animals with little or no interaction from the parents except to tell the children to get down from the fence, stop running, or tie their shoes.

The kind of visit just described is strictly recreational. But it could be an educational experience if the parents interacted directly with the children. It does not need to be a formal lecture or lesson. Make comments out loud while the children feed the animals. Ask the children thoughtful questions. This will help reinforce the names of the animals as well as develop other related vocabulary. The exchange below is an example of a meaningful and educational conversation at a farm.

> *Mom:* Look, Gina. That black goat is eating grass. He looks hungry. What are those things on top of the goat's head?
>
> *Gina:* They're sharp!
>
> *Mom:* That's right! Those sharp things are called horns. Horns are sharp. Do all these goats have horns?
>
> *Gina:* No. Those little ones don't have them.
>
> *Mom:* That's right. The little goats are baby goats called "kids." Kids don't have horns. Sometimes we call children "kids," too, don't we?
>
> *Gina:* Yeah, I'm a kid!
>
> *Mom:* You don't have horns, do you?
>
> *Gina:* (laughing) No! I'm not a goat; I'm a different kind of kid! I like the little brown one. Which goat do you like best, Mom?

Talking about what you see with your child while you see it is important. Simply exposing your child to places and experiences is only the first step in developing a well-rounded child. A parent must show personal interest in the event and provide the vocabulary necessary to describe and explain what you both are experiencing. Getting verbal feedback from your son or daughter not only shows that you have information to give to your child, but also shows that you are interested in your child's opinion, feelings, and observations. A conversation should always be a two-way discussion, not a lecture.

If visiting places such as a zoo or aquarium is financially or geographically out of the question, your local library can supply enough books to make you and your child feel like you've been there. Most libraries also loan videos for free, which can provide another good source for learning about everything from sharks to dinosaurs.

- *Answer questions completely.* Often a child will ask a question about how something operates, what the parts are, or why it does something. Even at the age of 2 to 3 years, children can absorb surprising amounts of information. By teaching them the specific words such as *van, station wagon,* and *jeep,* instead of just calling all vehicles *cars,* you can expand their vocabulary. Try to answer your child's questions in a straightforward manner, using vocabulary that is always a little ahead of the vocabulary the child presently uses.

This is *not* a helpful exchange:

Child (age 3½): Dad, where does a horse live?
Father: Oh, a horse lives in a place with other animals on a farm.
Child: Where on the farm?
Father: Inside, with other horses.

This father mistakenly assumed that since the child was familiar only with the word *farm,* it would be best to answer in words the child already knew and could understand.

This is a more helpful exchange:

Child: Dad, where does a horse live?
Father: Most horses live on farms. On a farm, there are big buildings called *barns.* Remember when we fed the cows near Aunt Sue's house? That big red building on the farm was a barn. The horses live inside the barn with other animals.
Child: Do they have kitchens and bathrooms?

Well, as you know, one good question often leads to several more! This father knew that his child would be able to process the information better if he could associate it with something familiar. If the child hadn't ever seen a barn, the father could draw one or find a picture of one. Understanding the new term *barn* then becomes much easier.

The next step is to manipulate the conversation to give the child the opportunity to say the new word *barn* as often as possible. Dad can say, "So the farmer puts the horses in a . . . what is that building called?" Encourage the child to use the word over and over so it eventually feels comfortable.

• *Talk about what you are doing.* Another helpful way to incorporate new words into your child's vocabulary is through "self-talk." Most parents do this when their child is very young but give it up as the child learns to talk. Self-talk means you narrate your own actions. Children with expressive vocabulary deficits not only need to hear the words used over and over by you but also need practice and encouragement to use the words themselves.

Following is an example of a self-talk exchange:

Parent: Brian, I'm measuring this flour to see if I have the right amount. Would you like to measure with me? The flour has to go all the way up to this line.

Brian: Okay.

Parent: (Puts in less than needed) Hmm . . . did I measure this correctly? Did it go all the way up to the line?

Brian: No, it's not enough.

Parent: You're right. I didn't measure it right, did I? Do you know what kind of cup this is? See, it has these lines on it so I can tell how much flour, sugar (or whatever I'm measuring) there is. It's a measuring cup. Do you remember what kind of cup this is?

Brian: A measuring cup.

Parent: Great! That's right. It's a measuring cup, and it's used for m . . . ?

Brian: Measuring.

Parent: What are some other things we could measure in this cup?

Notice how the parent continued to repeat the "new" word (measure) and elicited the use of the word from the child.

• *Help your prekindergartener learn about words and sounds.* A good way to facilitate language awareness in prekindergarten children is to help them begin to notice rhyming words and patterns. Dr. Seuss books, such as *Green Eggs and Ham* and *The Cat in the Hat,* and A. A. Milne's *Now We Are Six* are great for this. Your local librarian can help you find other appropriate books. Make up silly words that rhyme together; for example, "We're having 'bancake-pancakes.' " Make rhymes with the names of the people in your family.

Help your child begin to observe initial sound patterns. Does *horse* start the same way as *hat* or *boy?* Let's find some other things around the house that start like *horse.* What sound (it's not necessarily important to identify the letter *H* at this point) do we hear at the beginning of *horse?*

Case Study: Jake and Hutch

I recently visited the homes of two toddlers. One child, Hutch, is at 2½ a very verbal and inquisitive child. He delights in experiencing new things and is filled with questions and observations that belie his tender age.

He even makes up his own knock-knock jokes. Though his sentences and pronunciation are still evolving, what he is saying is clearly quite advanced for his age.

The other child, whom I'll call Jake, is slightly older. Jake is within normal limits for his age, but Jake doesn't have much to say. The questions he asks are more functional, such as "Can I have lunch now?" He doesn't show much interest or enthusiasm for books or new people. He spends most of his time playing on swings and slides. He seems disinterested in his surroundings and elaborates very little when answering questions. His vocabulary is noticeably less developed than Hutch's.

Were Hutch and Jake born with these traits, or was it the result of nurturing? Most experts agree that we are born with a certain amount of potential. Genes, prenatal care, and birth complications play a part in what a child has to work with from the start. If the right kind of stimulation does not occur, however, that potential shrinks over time. Jake and Hutch might have been born with the same potential, but even at their young ages, I could see that Hutch already had an edge over Jake.

What could be happening to cause the differences in Jake and Hutch? Certainly any parent will tell you that each child has a distinct personality from birth. Some children are just not talkative and never will be! Personalities aside, language and learning behaviors are greatly influenced by a child's environment.

Hutch's mother has a family membership to the zoo and aquarium, which they visit regularly. They go to the library each week. Hutch's father shows an interest in what Hutch says. Hutch's parents patiently respond to his questions with appropriate, complete answers. They all read books together; Hutch knows some by heart from hearing them so often. In addition to reading stories, Mom and Dad talk enthusiastically about them with Hutch. When they go somewhere, they explain where they are going, what they see, and why, why, why! It's no wonder Hutch has found it productive to talk. Someone he cares about, more than anyone, listens to him and values what he says. He has learned that it is fun to say new words and understand why.

Jake's mother finds it easier to let him play independently or with the other neighborhood children, because it keeps him busy. Jake and his brothers watch cartoon videos at home in rainy weather. Mom gives short, perfunctory answers to Jake's questions and lets him know with her tone of voice and facial expressions that he is bothering her with his trivial queries. After all, she has wash to do. It's important to keep his clothes clean, she tells me. They also go to the library, but Mom doesn't look at what Jake selects. She hastily takes the books for check-out and leaves them on his dresser at home. She figures he can look at them if he chooses. Sometimes she will quickly read one at night, but she grows impatient when Jake wants to hear it again or asks questions. There's too much to do, and his questions are fatiguing. Jake has figured this out, because he rarely asks them anymore, his mother says with a sigh of relief. At the dinner table, the children are urged to be quiet and eat.

Both sets of parents are doing what they think is best for their children. Jake and Hutch are each loved and adored by their parents. Both mothers are even able to stay at home full-time with their children. While Jake's house and clothes may be a slight bit more tidy, his intellectual development is not being stimulated as it could be. Jake may do okay once in school, but he could do much better if stimulated now.

It is important sometimes to let certain tasks go in order to take time with a child—time to talk, to explore, and to be good nurturers. Learning and language development is crucial in the first five to seven years. You can't, and shouldn't, wait for teachers in school to open up your child's mind to the world.

Whether this stimulation comes from a parent or caretaker, it must come from someone. And it must happen on an ongoing, day-in, day-out basis. A good day-care placement in a nurturing environment can be just as stimulating for language development as a parent. In Jake's case, he may have more opportunities for stimulation in a day-care situation because the baby-sitter or caretaker would not be as a distracted with household chores.

Language and learning can occur during even the simplest of daily activities, such as meal times, shopping, and while watching TV. But only if someone facilitates it. Bringing a child to a zoo is not teaching a child about a zoo if there is no exchange of information or parental enthusiasm about the adventure. If all your time is spent silently watching animals or catching up on news with adult friends, your child has gained little from the experience.

Reading a story about a funny monkey may not be exciting for you. Seeing an elephant eat hay or a hearing a horse neigh is probably "old-hat" for us grown-ups, too. But a child experiences these things with wonder and delight. When a parent shows interest and enthusiasm in these things, it tells the child, "I enjoy doing this with you. Learning about new things is fun. Asking questions is good." When a parent is disinterested and does not value learning, a child is being set up for a lifetime of mediocrity.

When Learning New Words Comes Slowly: Vocabulary Problems

*Sometimes I don't understand what Miss Rodriguez is talking about.
I've heard the words before, but I forget what they mean. When I have
to write my spelling words in sentences, I hate it! I kinda know what
they mean, but not exactly. When I read stories, I don't understand
what's going on. And when I take tests in class, I forget everything.
All the names and places start to sound the same. Maybe my teacher
is right; if I really tried, I could do better.*

—Janet, age 10

Probably the most common trait found in children with language problems is the inability to understand or use words correctly. Our **vocabulary** represents the bank of words we use and whose meanings we understand. Janet is an example of a typical child with a language delay or disorder. She may have had difficulty learning to speak or putting sentences together as a toddler, or perhaps she did not show any sign of a language problem at all.

Understanding and using words is an important part of language development. Many children with language problems have difficulty learning or comprehending words, which is why it is usually one of the first areas a speech-language pathologist evaluates when testing.

Children like Janet are easy to miss. Typically, the brighter the student, the less likely it is someone will think there is a problem. Also, if the student is older, a parent or teacher is apt to think that someone would have found the problem, if there was one, by this age. Janet's speech probably sounds normal, and she may be a very bright girl. However, something is getting in the way of her learning and classwork. In this section, you will learn how to recognize and understand a child with Janet's problem and what can be done for children like her.

Difficulty Understanding Words: A Receptive Vocabulary Problem

Receptive vocabulary refers to all the words a child understands. Whether the child ever uses the words is a different matter. Receptive vocabulary is probably one of the most important language skill areas assessed. After all, children won't speak or write with words they don't understand. They can't accurately follow directions, written or verbal, if they don't know what the words mean. They can't understand what they are reading if the words don't make sense. If a child has this problem, we call it a *receptive vocabulary deficit, receptive vocabulary delay,* or *receptive vocabulary weakness.*

Difficulty with receptive vocabulary can have a serious impact on a child's academic achievement and should not be taken lightly. It is also probably one of the most critical areas in which a parent needs to take an active and aggressive role on a day-to-day basis.

When a baby is acquiring a receptive vocabulary, parents often play verbal games with picture books, asking questions such as "Can you show me the boat?" and "Where's the cow?" These are helpful and fun games, but they also let you know that your child is making the important connection between a word and the object it represents. Children can usually do this before they can name the picture itself. In fact, asking children to point to the picture is a good way to prepare them to say the word later on.

If you refer your child for a language evaluation, you can expect that the child will be given a receptive vocabulary test. To find out which words your child understands, the speech-language pathologist will probably ask the child to point to a particular picture with a set of four pictures to choose from. Often children with receptive vocabulary difficulties know *something* about the word, but they don't know it very well. For example, a 6-year-old boy may know a goat is a farm animal, but when a picture of a goat is shown next to a sheep or ram, he becomes confused. He vaguely knows *goat,* but he doesn't know it specifically. A 10-year-old girl may know that a *fossil* has something to do with age and rocks, so she may assume that all old rocks are fossils. She knows *fossil,* vaguely, but she doesn't know it exactly. The age at which a child is expected to really know a given word has been determined by researchers studying hundreds and thousands of children.

Receptive vocabulary encompasses all types of words, not just the name of objects. These are the word groups typically examined:

- Nouns, identifying a person, place, or thing, such as *table*
- Adjectives, words used to describe, such as *tall*
- Verbs, action words, such as *jumping*
- Prepositions, positional words, such as *below*
- Adverbs, telling how something is done, such as *quickly*

Therefore, when a child has difficulty *using* words, a speech-language pathologist will first want to know if that child is *comprehending* the meaning of words with accuracy. Receptive vocabulary weaknesses (deficits) are often at the heart of expressive vocabulary problems. You can't say or use words you don't fully understand, can you?

How Does a Receptive Vocabulary Deficit Affect a Child?

Difficulty in understanding or remembering the meaning of words can make a person feel isolated and confused. Imagine waking up in a foreign country with only a minimal knowledge of the language. People speak to you, perhaps ask questions or make requests, but you're not sure what all the words mean. You may try to follow along or guess the meaning because everyone expects you should know what they are talking about. Consider this exchange in the classroom from the point of view of Heather, a student with a receptive vocabulary deficit:

> *Teacher:* Class, today since our bordet of sool is harvent, I would like all of you to plen and let the others jess. Now, Heather, what is the barnish there?
> *Heather:* Uh, I'm not sure.
> *Teacher:* Were you listening? Hmm . . . maybe someone can help Heather out . . . Allison?

Think of how exhausting it would be to follow a discussion with so many bits and pieces missing!

Eventually a child may tune out or cover up confusion by making a joke out of it. Since social conversations are sometimes confusing, the child begins to avoid them. The child may prefer other ways of making friends, such as through sports. On a soccer field, most communication is nonverbal and is thus much easier to understand. It feels great for any child to be "one of the gang."

In the course of an everyday conversation, the problems may not be apparent for a child with a mild problem, but in the classroom, new vocabulary terms are introduced every day. Most tests are structured to see how many terms a child understands. Think of a typical science or social studies test. They are filled with matching columns, fill-in-the-blanks, and true/false. What does a child do when the words all become a blur when presented side by side? Typically, such children perform poorly on tests and lose the incentive to study, which in turn is blamed as the source of the problem. Whenever students tell me they study but can't pass the tests, I make sure their vocabulary skills are evaluated thoroughly.

Receptive vocabulary weaknesses also affect reading comprehension, requiring the child to rely on pictures and context clues to discern the meaning of the words. This often suffices in the early grades but eventually may be overwhelming due to the amount of reading involved in social studies, science, and other subject areas in later grades.

Attention span during oral discussions is often affected because the child has to piece together the meaning of so many words that it is all but impossible to follow along for long periods of time.

Children who continue to be two years or more behind their peers in receptive vocabulary skills by middle or high school will surely struggle in college. As an adult, understanding what people say is also important for understanding news events discussed on TV, social conversations, and work-related tasks. Someone who continues to have low receptive vocabulary skills as an adult will probably have better success in occupations that require less intense conversation such as computer programming, plumbing, carpentry, and other hands-on fields.

Difficulty Using Words: An Expressive Vocabulary Problem

If a child has difficulty finding or knowing the most appropriate words to use when speaking, we call this an *expressive vocabulary deficit.* It can also be called an *expressive vocabulary weakness* or *expressive vocabulary delay.* This can be observed when the child is naming an object or picture, expressing emotions, retelling a story, or describing someone or something.

A child with an expressive vocabulary problem often uses general or vague terms instead of specific words. For example, when asked to describe a boy sledding in a blizzard, a fifth-grade student with an expressive vocabulary problem might say, "It's a boy riding down the hill. He has winter clothes on. It's bad outside."

This description may be appropriate at the kindergarten or first-grade level, but by fifth grade, most children have acquired a *working*, active vocabulary to more accurately describe that scene. In most cases, the child may indeed understand or recognize the concepts in question. ("Is there a blizzard in this picture?" "Yes.") The difference is the words have not become incorporated into the child's everyday language at the age one would expect.

If the words are punctuated by a lot of "ums," "uhs," and "whatchamacallits," there may be a word retrieval problem contributing to the vocabulary deficit as well. Later in this chapter, word retrieval problems are discussed in greater detail. If your child has been diagnosed with an expressive language deficit, a word retrieval problem may be part of the overall profile because it often goes hand-in-hand with expressive language delays.

Semantics, as mentioned in chapter 3, is how we use the words we know. For example, children often say, "I was bitten by a bee." It's not that children haven't heard or don't know *stung,* but the subtle differences in meanings are still not clear. They may say a building is *big,* when they really mean *tall,* or they may say their bug bite is *scratchy* instead of *itchy.* These misuses of words are a normal part of development for children. However, in time a child should be able to use the correct forms more readily. When a child has vocabulary deficits and/or word retrieval problems, semantic skills are compromised.

Some children are good at naming pictures in isolation but don't use the words in the correct context in conversation during certain language tasks, such as the following:

- Using synonyms (words with similar meanings)
- Using antonyms (opposites)
- Defining words
- Using words with multiple meanings
- Classifying words into categories
- Using words in sentences

How Does an Expressive Vocabulary Weakness Affect a Child?

If your child is still using "baby talk" beyond the age of 3 or 4 to refer to many people and objects (but is able to imitate the proper word reasonably well when prompted), it may be due to an expressive vocabulary deficit.

This problem would show up academically during most verbal activities in the early primary grades. Often teachers use Show and Tell and hands-on activities with the children to facilitate language and vocabulary growth. As a class, they discuss what they saw and did. Children with expressive vocabulary difficulties often neglect to use the new words when they retell these events.

A current trend is toward using the "whole-language" approach to teach reading and writing skills in the early elementary grades. This approach emphasizes facilitating a child's interest in words using commercial books, rather than textbooks, and helping them write stories that are of interest to them. With this approach, children are no longer constrained from expressing themselves by the mechanics of skills they have not yet learned, such as advanced spelling or punctuation. Unfortunately, children with expressive vocabulary deficits may not possess the words to utilize whole language as other children do, and they may need help from the teacher to vary and expand the number of words they use in their oral and written language. With proper modifications, therapy, and consultation, the whole-language approach offers a very effective way to improve vocabulary skills in the classroom.

When a child with an expressive vocabulary deficit writes sentences or stories, the sentence structures may seem dull, repetitive, or short due to the limited pool of words the child draws from. For example, when asked to write these words in a sentence—*sun, seal, seat*—a child in second or third grade with an expressive vocabulary problem may write: *I see the sun. I see the seal. I have a seat.* It's not that the child doesn't know that the sun is yellow, is in the sky, and that it gives us light or warmth, it's just that using or thinking of the words is difficult.

In reading activities, a child with an expressive vocabulary deficit may have no difficulty understanding the content or vocabulary in the story. However, when asked to define or use new words in isolation, the child may have problems. This difficulty carries over into social studies or science as well.

Children are bombarded with new terms in school. Those with an expressive vocabulary problem may be able to study long and hard enough to pass tests that show they know these words, but without regular conscious use and repetition, these words may never be comfortable or familiar enough for them to use in their speaking vocabulary. A child with an expressive vocabulary problem needs lots and lots of practice using new words.

At home there may be some confusion or frustration in communicating with a child whose expressive vocabulary is very limited. A 5-year-old child with this problem may say excitedly, "Mom, you said I could have that candy-thing! I left it back there on that table next to the stuff, and now it's broke and I won't have the right color!" After you play Twenty Questions, you may find out that the "candy-thing" is a candy cane, it's cracked (not broken), and the child was afraid the other sibling was going to get the red piece!

As for the future, a child with limited expressive vocabulary skills can probably slip by unnoticed by most outside the classroom unless the problem is somewhat severe. The child's writing and speaking may seem dull, because words are repetitive and not terribly varied. A child with an expressive vocabulary problem would not make a good writer but, with a little bit of effort, should be able to learn whatever words he needs to learn.

Characteristics of Children with Receptive or Expressive Vocabulary Problems

Children age 3 or older who have receptive or expressive vocabulary weaknesses might do the following:

- Express displeasure by crying, hitting, or other acting out behaviors instead of explaining the problem or feelings with words

- Supplement talking with much more gesturing and sound effects than a typical child would
- Hold on to baby talk, calling objects by a name they create even though capable of saying the correct word
- Perform poorly on tests; forget new terms quickly
- Watch what other children do for cues
- Describe and tell stories with vague language
- Overgeneralize words; for example, refer to all flowers as *roses*
- Have difficulty with categories; for example, refer to jewelry and clothing as *stuff to put on*
- Have difficulty with synonyms, antonyms, and words with multiple meanings
- Retreat from social conversations and lectures in class
- Experience difficulty with reading comprehension
- Miss the point of classroom discussions
- Perform well in school in the primary grades but have increasing difficulty after the second grade
- Know the words in a vague sort of way but not fully understand the exact meaning
- Make up words such as *a car loader truck* or a *twisty plant that goes up the house* even after the correct word has been heard many times
- Use words that are similar to, but not as precise in meaning as, the appropriate word ("We went to uh . . . that sandy place on Saturday.")

What Can Parents Do to Help a Child with a Receptive or Expressive Vocabulary Weakness?

The good news is, you can do much to improve your child's vocabulary. Individualized therapy in isolation has little or no impact on your child's receptive or expressive vocabulary unless constant and regular reinforcement occurs at home. Unfortunately, there is no quick fix. For preschoolers, you will need to take an active role in expanding your child's vocabulary. Your child's speech pathologist can give you many suggestions as to how this can best be incorporated into your day-to-day life. Once in school, children have opportunities all day to learn new words, but your continued support and reinforcement will be important. A child with a receptive or expressive vocabulary delay will need lots of repetition and practice using these words in order for them to "stick." This is where you come in! As I've said before, words are learned best when a child has a reason to know them and many opportunities to use them. If your child has been diagnosed with a receptive or expressive vocabulary deficit, here are some suggestions for you:

- Have a *tympanogram* and pure-tone screening test done by an audiologist (your ear, nose, and throat doctor can direct you to one), pediatrician, or school nurse to ensure that there is no fluid lingering in the middle ear or a hearing problem.
- Talk to your child about everything; explain, discuss, and answer questions with patience and clarity.
- Try to be precise in your own use of language around the child.
- Use new words over and over in many different contexts.
- If your child can read, put the new word in writing in as many different ways as possible.
- Make a picture book; cut out pictures from magazines and catalogs and practice naming them together.
- Offer choices when trying to elicit descriptive language. For example: "Timmy, does that orange taste sweet or salty?"
- Help your child learn the names of categories and what kinds of words belong in them, such as *furniture, jewelry,* and *fruits.*
- Play games where you describe things you see as you drive, with as many words as possible, such as *tall, striped, soft,* and *furry.*
- Make sure the classroom teachers are aware of your child's problem, and work with the speech pathologist.
- Read stories out loud to your child and discuss them together.

It is important to find out whether other factors are contributing to the deficit. Children scoring significantly below their peers may have subtle or temporary hearing problems. Their vocabulary may not readily improve unless the hearing problem is medically treated. Other contributing factors may include lack of stimulation in the language tested (if a foreign language is spoken frequently at home) or auditory memory problems (listening disorders). Children with mental retardation do have depressed expressive and receptive vocabulary scores as well, but language is one of many skills that are assessed to make this determination. A diagnosis such as this is made by a team of specialists. Your speech-language pathologist will be able to tell you if your child needs additional testing.

Case Study: Angelique

Angelique was referred to me by her classroom teacher when she was in third grade. She was doing very well in math, art, music, physical educa-

tion, spelling, language arts, and writing. Her problems were in reading comprehension, social studies, and science. Her teacher was also concerned because Angelique seemed to make irrelevant comments during class discussions. Sometimes she confused the class because she would speak in vague terms and use words incorrectly. When completing homework assignments, she took a long time to answer questions that required her to identify and explain new vocabulary words. Sometimes even understanding the question itself was difficult for Angelique. If Angelique studied long and hard, she was able to pass tests, but the marathon study sessions were taking their toll. Considering Angelique's As and Bs in other subjects, the Cs and Ds in reading, social studies, and science seemed suspicious.

In Angelique's case, she did not avoid social conversations. In fact, she was a bubbly and outgoing girl.

Angelique had initially been referred to remedial services in January of her second-grade year for extra help in reading comprehension. This small-group instruction had been helpful and had improved her vocabulary. Unfortunately, new words introduced in school outpaced these half-hour sessions held twice a week. Besides, many of the words in these supplemental classes were taught in addition to the ones piling up from her other classes. Without repetition and practice, the words became more and more of a blur. So by the time Angelique reached third grade, she was further behind her classmates.

Angelique's third-grade teacher made the referral to the Child Study Team in April. After discussing Angelique's case, the team decided to have the school's learning disabilities specialist speak to the teacher and observe Angelique in class. Discussions with Angelique's mother confirmed the inordinate amount of time and effort required for Angelique to complete certain homework activities and study for tests. In May, an evaluation was performed by the learning disabilities consultant and psychologist. There were no perceptual problems or emotional issues demonstrated that could explain these difficulties. Angelique's ability for nonverbal tasks was somewhat higher than for verbal tasks, although both scores placed her solidly in the average range.

However, both examiners did notice that Angelique would often ask to have the test questions explained because she "didn't know what she was supposed to do." She misunderstood several of the tasks, but she could complete them satisfactorily when shown a few practice examples. When she spoke, her language was vague. The psychologist recalled Angelique complimenting the "bottom dress" (skirt) the psychologist was wearing and placing her pencil "inside the pens" (between). Due to these observations, a speech-language evaluation was requested.

Since it was the end of the year, I administered the evaluation over

the course of several weeks the following September when Angelique be-
gan fourth grade. It showed that Angelique had clear deficits in receptive
and expressive vocabulary, as well as difficulty in related semantic skills.
After a meeting in October, I recommended that Angelique attend small-
group therapy twice a week to work on these skills and other areas that
were also affected. In addition to the therapy, and no less important, were
the modifications in the classroom that took place. These were carried out
by Angelique's classroom teacher, with assistance and periodic consulta-
tion from me. By prioritizing and limiting vocabulary lists and assignments
as well as restructuring tests to accommodate her weaknesses, Angelique
was able to have a successful fourth-grade year.

You should note that it took several months to find the root of
Angelique's problems. This is not an uncommon scenario; indeed, it is a
typical, rather than idealized, picture of what often happens to children
like Angelique in a public school system. The delay between the initial
referral and the time treatment begins is frustrating. The bureaucracy and
legal requirements make much of this unavoidable. You can help, however, by letting your child's teacher know whether completing homework
or studying requires extraordinary amounts of your child's time and energy or whether your child consistently resists doing the assignments unless you sit and help with each question. Children sometimes seem to
cope well in the classroom but fall apart at home. Good communication
between home and school can get the process moving more quickly and
bring about solutions and strategies to allow your child to succeed and
enjoy school.

The "Him Not Talkin' Right" Child: Morphological and Syntax Problems

I not goin' school today, Mommy. I sick. We goin' a doctor? Why you
take me to doctor Mommy? Him give me shot? Maybe yesterday I
jump around too much. Tommy falled off and he have two cut now.
I won' jump anymore.

—Pete, age 6

When Pete talks, his problem may be noticeable to you. However, for a
parent who sees Pete every day, it's easy to get used to the way he talks
and simply accept it as "something he'll grow out of." As we discussed
in the first two chapters, Pete's speech is a bit behind his 6-year-old peers.

In fact, his problem is more correctly described as an expressive language problem as opposed to an articulation deficit, because he is capable of pronouncing the words he is not using correctly. Also, he may not grow out of it, particularly if he doesn't get the right kind of help.

If Pete were a 2-year-old or a young 3-year-old, we wouldn't characterize him as having a speech problem. But he's 6 now and still retains a babyish quality to the way he puts words and sentences together. If your child speaks this way and has already turned 4, he or she may need help to learn to speak correctly.

All children (and adults, for that matter) have difficulty with certain aspects of grammar. Did he play that song *good* or *well?* Would you like to come with *John and me?* Or come with *John and I?* These are typical problems everyone wrestles with as they develop language. Children may say *goin'* instead of *going.* Adolescents use certain words and phrases that are "hip" to their culture and may sound quite foreign to us dinosaurs. However, these are different issues from children who genuinely cannot put their thoughts together in a simple, grammatically correct sentence.

In this section, I'll explain the kinds of grammar problems children may exhibit, how children are affected, and what parents can do to help.

Pete's kind of speech pattern actually is symptomatic of a language delay in two areas (morphology and syntax), but they typically go hand in hand, so I've included both in this section.

Morphological Deficits

A child with a **morphological deficit** has difficulty using the correct endings with words, which is a type of expressive language problem. The English language is filled with endings that change meaning. We change verbs by adding an ending to show present tense ("plays" or "play*ing*") or past tense ("play*ed*"). We use *s* to show something belongs to someone ("Daddy*'s* tie") and that there is more than one of something ("Six cars"). When we use contractions ("I*'ll*"), the part following the apostrophe also serves as an ending. Of course, there are many exceptions to the rules in the English language, so you can expect a child who is already not quite clear with word rules to have difficulty with any words that don't follow the rules as well.

Most of us are fortunate enough to learn grammar rules simply by listening to others speak and imitating what we hear. It is not a conscious or direct process. For some children though, it doesn't work this way.

Fluctuating hearing loss from frequent ear infections is a common cause of morphological errors, because endings are mostly high-pitched sounds that may not be heard when the ear is filled with fluid. Children will say words the way they hear them. Sometimes children with severe articulation problems leave off endings because it is physically hard for them to make the necessary sounds. Some children may be unaware of how their speech sounds to others, or they may have yet to learn the rules. Children whose overall development is delayed may also have difficulty learning morphological rules and speaking correctly.

Syntax Deficits

Syntax refers to the order of the words in a sentence. A **syntax deficit** is another type of expressive language problem. When babies and toddlers first learn to speak, they use phrases and shortened sentences with incorrect syntax. As with morphological deficits, Pete should be using more grammatically correct sentences by the age of 6. Some children omit entire words (as well as endings) or put them in the wrong order. A child with a syntax problem may phrase a question the same way as a statement ("We goin' a doctor?") but add the proper inflection at the end of the sentence to let you know he would like an answer. Other times, only the important words in a sentence are used, omitting articles, *is,* prepositions, and so forth. For example, a child with delayed syntax might say, "Richie kick ball."

Characteristics of Children with Grammar Problems

Children with morphological or syntax problems might do the following:

- Use the wrong pronoun (e.g., say "Him over there" instead of "He is over there.")
- Omit words at the beginning of a question (e.g., say "You have candy?" instead of "Do you have candy?")
- Omit the word or contraction for *is* in sentences (e.g., say "It cold" instead of "It's cold" or "It is cold.")
- Confuse *has* and *have* (e.g., say "Mommy have a cold" instead of "Mommy has a cold.")
- Omit articles *a, an,* and *the* or use them incorrectly (e.g., say "I have balloon" instead of "I have a balloon.")
- Omit endings for past tense verbs (e.g., say "I jump over it" instead of "I jumped over it.")
- Omit endings that show the possessive form of a noun (e.g., say "Mommy shirt is blue" instead of "Mommy's shirt is blue.")

- Omit endings that show plurals (e.g., say "three car" instead of "three cars.")
- Overgeneralize regular verb rules to irregular verbs (e.g., say "I gived the doll a bath" instead of "I gave the doll a bath.")

Note: Many "normal" children persist in using the incorrect form of a few irregular verbs into the first grade or so. It's a problem only when it is pervasive, consistent, and in a child older than 5 or so.

How Do Grammar Problems Affect a Child?

Most people can understand the message Pete is trying to communicate, despite his awkward use of words and sentences. In this respect, Pete is less apt to be frustrated or unable to form social relationships because of the speech problem. However, the older a child gets, the more noticeable the problem becomes. Sometimes other children and adults draw the conclusion that a child who speaks this way is "slow."

As children begin to learn to write sentences and stories in school, they need to rely on that "inner voice" we all have to decide which words to write and how to write them. If Pete says "I happy," that is what he will write. Children who have difficulty internalizing language rules for speaking may also have problems with other language rules needed for reading and writing.

Most children of normal intelligence are able to overcome any problems with grammar if they receive the appropriate therapy. Some children may choose to ignore grammatical rules to fit in with a particular group or culture, but this tends to be voluntary and not a true disorder.

What Can Parents Do to Help a Child with Grammar Problems?

It is very important to get professional help for a child like Pete because a speech pathologist will be able to zero in on *one* skill at a time to work on. Each of the skills listed earlier may require weeks or even months of concentrated therapy and practice before your child can be ready to try to incorporate it into his or her conversational speech. The speech pathologist can guide you with activities to do at home and share ideas about how to reward and praise your child for using the correct skill, as opposed to making the child feel inadequate when he or she forgets. Here are some more suggestions:

- Don't attempt to help children speak better by asking them to repeat sentences correctly after you when they speak incorrectly. When you focus so much attention on *how* your son or daughter is speaking and not on *what* is being said, you can unintentionally discourage your child from trying to talk to you at all. Also, in a child's mind, "Mommy doesn't like it when I say it this way" can be easily translated to "Mommy doesn't like me."

• Listen to what your child says, and then respond by rephrasing what was said, using the correct words and sentence structure. Emphasizing the missing words or endings helps, too. This "mirroring" also lets your child know you received the message. Here is an example of a helpful exchange between Pete and his father:

> *Pete:* Daddy, we goin' a Gramma house today?
> *Father: Are* we going to Grandma's house today? Yes, after lunch we'll get ready to go.
> *Pete:* Melissa goin' too?
> *Father:* Yes, Melissa *is* going too.
> *Pete:* Her sittin' in the back seat, right?
> *Father:* Yes, *she's* sitting in the back seat.

• Use a patient, relaxed, and interested tone of voice when speaking with your child. Expressing impatience or dismay with the way she speaks can only make things worse.

• Find the time to work with your child at home if the speech pathologist sends home specific activities to do. Make it a priority. The more diligent you are about the exercises, the faster your child will progress.

Case Study: Jacob

Jacob was referred to me by his mother for a speech-language evaluation when he was 4½. She was concerned because Jacob was going to start kindergarten in nine months, and he was still "talking like a baby."

Working as a private practitioner on this case, I was able to schedule the testing the same week his mother called. When Jacob arrived for the evaluation, he was somewhat shy and reluctant to talk. He clung to his mother and hid behind her skirt. Using puppets and stuffed animals, I eventually elicited a quick smile and a few words. "He talks much more than this, really!" his exasperated mother told me. Not to worry. Any speech pathologist worth his or her salt knows it takes some time to draw out young children and win their confidence. The evaluation proceeded smoothly over the course of two or three sessions.

Jacob had very strong vocabulary skills and exhibited no difficulty following directions or comprehending what was said to him. He was, however, somewhat distractible for his age and clearly exhibited difficulty putting sentences together and using the correct forms of words. I wrote down what he said and counted the average number of words per "utterance," a technique called **MLU** *(mean length of utterance), which showed the quantity as well as the quality of his language was a bit delayed. In addition, Jacob had some minor pronunciation problems that, along with his syntax and morphological errors, led me to suspect a possible hearing problem.*

When I reviewed Jacob's medical and developmental history with his mother, she mentioned he had had several nasty and persistent ear infections in the past two years. "But he's fine now. He hasn't had a fever or complained of pain in a few months. Besides, I know he's hearing me because he answers me when I ask him questions. Unless of course he's in front of the TV, then I might as well be a potted plant. You know how kids are!"

If you've read the first few chapters, you can probably guess where Jacob went next. That's right, I sent him to the ear, nose, and throat doctor for a hearing evaluation by the audiologist on staff at the office. Guess what the hearing test showed? Jacob had a mild hearing loss, which affected his ability to hear higher frequencies, as well as residual fluid behind his eardrum causing speech to sound somewhat muffled or distorted to him. Jacob was placed on antihistamines to dry up the fluid and antibiotics to cure the mild infection that was persisting. At a later testing, he still had fluid present in the middle ear and a mild hearing loss. Because it was a persistent and unresponsive condition, Jacob had tubes put in about two months after my initial evaluation.

In the meantime, I began a speech-language therapy program with Jacob. He came twice a week for individual sessions, and his parents worked consistently with the activities I gave them to do at home. By the time Jacob began kindergarten, he was speaking much more clearly. We also worked on some listening skills, which were weak in a few areas. By the time Jacob finished his kindergarten, he was speaking at age level about 90–100% of the time. He was phased out of speech-language therapy and has recently graduated from high school with honors. (Where does the time go?)

The "Whatchamacallit, um, Thing Over There" Child: A Word Retrieval Problem

Sometimes when I try to think of what I want to say, uh . . . the words get um . . . jumbled up in my head. . . . When the teacher calls on me in class, I can't think of it fast enough, so uh . . . I just say "I don't know." I wish I wasn't so stupid.

—Jared, age 9

Have you ever momentarily forgotten a word? Well, it's a very common phenomenon we all experience from time to time. Sometimes it may even be a fairly simple word that escapes you. It's a frustrating feeling, because you *know* you know this word. You may even "see" some of the letters in your mind, which helps your brain search through its files and pull the word you want. Sometimes you resort to selecting a word with a similar meaning to get past the awkward pause in the conversation. But you probably still wrack your brain until minutes later it usually magically appears.

Just like adults, when children have words inside that don't come out on cue, it can be frustrating and confusing. A child with a *word retrieval deficit* (also called a **word-finding problem**) experiences that all too uh . . . um . . . common feeling we all get from time to time, but on a much more frequent basis. Sometimes the initial sound of a word is on the tip of the tongue; other times nothing at all comes into mind. This is a type of expressive language problem.

Jared describes how it feels to have a word retrieval problem. In this section we'll go over how to recognize and understand a child with Jared's problem and examine what can be done for children like him.

Word retrieval deficits refer to the brain's inability to pull words from its "file" quickly enough to use in the desired context. We all have moments throughout the day where our brain thinks of an idea to communicate to another person before our language center has properly pulled the words we will use. We start talking and expect that "we'll think of it" by the time we get to it. By saying "um," we give ourselves that extra second or two to get our thoughts organized.

When I recently visited Japan, I was struck by the frequent use of the word *ano* in Japanese conversations. In my studies of Japanese from tapes and textbooks, I had not come across that word in the context it was being used. It was interesting for me to find out that *ano* is the Japanese equivalent of *um*. In England, people tend to use *emm* when stalling. So you see, we humans do need some time to retrieve our words.

When children experience word retrieval problems, their ability to think of the words they want to say is much more impaired than adults' momentary lapses. Even a few well-placed *ums* are usually not enough to cover the time they need to think of the word. When a child has a word-finding problem, it is often perceived as a problem with vocabulary. However, a true word retrieval problem is *not* caused by a lack of exposure to a word. The child has heard the word many times and perhaps even used it on other occasions without difficulty. The word is "in there," but the child just can't get it out when it's needed.

Bona fide word retrieval problems are difficult to diagnose in young children because they are still learning new words. All children will grope for words and misuse them in conversation. But by the age of 7 or 8, children should be more fluent in their speech and not grope for simple words they've used before. This is why, in the absence of other obvious speech or learning problems, word retrieval problems are often overlooked until the elementary or secondary school years.

Therapy for a Child with a Word Retrieval Problem

How does our brain's storage system work? Think of when you were stuck, trying to remember the name of a recent acquaintance. Was it Janet or Joan? You remember her last name began with a *B*. These are the clues you give yourself to work with, as you try to "find" the woman's name. Ah! Judi Benton, that's it. Many times, we use the sounds or letters in someone's name to help get us started. It may take a few minutes, but it often works.

To "file" a word correctly, people must perceive the word's sounds and parts accurately. For example, if Jared pronounces the word *expected* quickly and without thought, it sometimes sounds like he's saying *esspected*. Other times it comes out as *spected* or *axspected*. This vagueness and lack of clarity makes it difficult for him to mentally pull the word out on demand. How does that word start again? Was it an *ess* at the beginning or *axe?* Therapy for children with word retrieval problems, therefore, often seeks to improve the child's understanding of a word's sounds and parts, developing a mental filing system for new words in this manner.

Since, in a pinch, a child may need to use a word with similar meaning in place of the desired word, therapy also focuses on expanding the child's existing vocabulary. By having more words to choose from, it is felt the child can compensate and work around the words that are momentarily stuck.

Still other therapy focuses on having the child use specific words and language in as many contexts as possible in order for the words to come more easily when needed.

Characteristics of Children with Word Retrieval Problems

When children are developing their language skills, it is quite common for them to grope or struggle when trying to think of a word. Don't be concerned unless it is a consistent problem or begins to interfere in daily conversation or classwork. This kind of problem is often difficult for an untrained person to detect and may only come to a parent's attention after an evaluation has been performed. Also, as mentioned previously, it is not uncommon for word retrieval problems to go undetected until a child is in upper elementary grades or older.

Children with word retrieval problems might:

- Possess average or above-average intellectual ability
- Sometimes exhibit other learning disabilities, often related to reading problems
- Use an inordinate amount of *ums, uhs,* or other stalls
- Exhibit grimacing, clenching of fists, blinking of eyes, or other shows of frustration when stalling
- Overuse vague words such as *stuff* and *thing* (e.g., "Put that thing on that other thing.")
- Use words that are similar to, but not as precise in meaning as, the intended word (e.g., "We went to uh . . . that sandy place on Saturday.")
- Talk around a subject or word instead of identifying it directly (e.g., "Oh, it's one of those things that you wear in your ear. It's jewelry.")
- Make up words such as *a car loader truck* or a *twisty plant that goes up the house,* particularly after they have already been exposed to the correct word and used it on many occasions
- Have difficulty pronouncing multisyllabic words; often mispronouncing or omitting syllables (e.g., *veggables* for *vegetables, atainer* for *container*)
- Have difficulty completing fill-in-the-blank test formats quickly or accurately
- Complete multiple-choice or matching-column test formats with greater success
- Need extra time to put thoughts together

- Raise their hand in class but often have no answer when called upon

How Does a Word Retrieval Problem Affect a Child?

A child like Jared will tend to speak in a roundabout way. He may describe something with very little detail or use vague language. This is how Jared described his family to me:

> *I have a very nice mother who goes there to uh . . . um . . . her work— job, I mean. I forget the name of her company. She is in charge of taking those things that you see on TV and putting them into these little, little, uh . . . OH! You know. Those things. She does that, but only on certain times. My Dad drives all the way up the big highway, every day, in his car. Well, it's not a regular car, it's one of those big ones, you know what I mean. A . . . I forget!*

When I showed Jared a picture of a van, he easily identified it as a van. He then said, "That's what my father drives, you know, a van. I just couldn't think of it." Jared hears the word *van* on an almost daily basis, according to his mother. But in this conversation, Jared couldn't get it out.

This may or may not present a problem for Jared in social situations as a child. Most children are not as critical or observant about this kind of a problem as adults are. However, if Jared is excited, and he's trying to tell another child a story or explain something that happened, he may have to answer a lot of questions. At home, you may also have to play Twenty Questions sometimes in order to get to the bottom of what your child with a word-finding problem is trying to tell you.

Although this problem is frustrating at times, it is usually a more subtle language problem than others covered in this book in terms of the effect on your child's life on a day-to-day basis outside the classroom. The real challenge for a child with a word retrieval problem is *in* the classroom. The child's teacher may get very confusing messages from the child, which can lead the teacher to a mistaken conclusion. Consider this exchange in the classroom with Dimitri, a boy with a word-finding problem:

> *Teacher:* Dimitri, what is the name of the planet closest to the sun?
> *Dimitri:* It's . . . uh . . .
> *Teacher:* Dimitri, did you do last night's assignment?
> *Dimitri:* Yes!

Teacher: Well, then, what is this planet's name?
Dimitri: Uh . . . it's that little planet that's so hot; it's not Pluto or
    Venus . . . it's uh . . .
Teacher: Can someone help Dimitri?

Anytime a teacher tells me a student is having diffficulty passing tests, particularly when the child seems to know and understand the words in other contexts, I look for a possible word retrieval problem. Standardized tests are available for this purpose, but often the problem can be noticed by listening to the way the child responds to casual conversational questions. I usually use a combination of formal tests and observation to make this diagnosis.

One reason taking tests is so difficult for children with this type of problem is that the information tested generally is new. Since children with a word retrieval deficit need to use words over and over before they can be retrieved successfully from the brain's files, they have difficulty with new information. For this reason, it is wise to limit the number of names, places, events, and vocabulary terms children like Dimitri must be expected to memorize at one time. When their brain becomes "overloaded," the words become a blur. This is particularly true if the words have not been used with any regularity. Dimitri's teacher should try to prioritize the words that are most important for him to learn and have him focus on those.

Because Dimitri's brain takes a little longer to find the information he is looking for, it helps if his teachers and parents show extra patience by waiting at least ten full seconds before asking him to respond to a question. The stress Dimitri feels to come up with an answer, *any* answer, will not help his brain function with any greater accuracy. In fact, timed tests and pressure for "fast answers" are extra obstacles for children like Dimitri.

Traditionally, many classroom tests use the time-honored fill-in-the-blank format. These open-ended questions are deadly for children like Dimitri. To try to remember a whole set of obscure words is torturous. If a child with this problem *does* do well, it may be at a very high cost: hours and hours of studying and assistance from you. Marathon study sessions take their toll on a family, as well as the child. This is compounded if the child would like to participate in sports or music (in which such a child may excel and should certainly participate) and not spend *all* free time studying to pass tests.

Often children like Dimitri are so overwhelmed by these types of tests that they stop trying or feel "stupid." By simply adding a list of words to choose from at the top of the test paper (referred to by teachers as a "word bank"), scores can literally go from a *C* or *D* to an *A* or *B*. This is one of the modifications discussed in chapter 4 that a child with an IEP could have incorporated into the school day. I have seen dramatic improvements in test scores with this little change alone. By changing the way the test is presented, the teacher can find out what the child *really* knows, and the child can be proud of a score that is a more accurate reflection of her knowledge. Imagine, such a simple, no-cost solution with such a tremendous return!

What Can Parents Do to Help a Child with a Word Retrieval Problem?

If you suspect your child has a word retrieval deficit, pursue an evaluation. Then, if your child is diagnosed by a speech-language pathologist as having a word retrieval (or word-finding) problem, keep these thoughts in mind:

- Be patient. Don't show frustration with your child's struggling.
- Give your child extra time to respond (e.g., say "After I finish unloading the dishwasher, can you tell me about your trip to the hardware store with Dad?")
- Recognize that the problem will probably not ever completely disappear; accept it as one small part of your child's unique personality.
- If your child is struggling and you think you know the word she is searching for, offer the initial sound (e.g., "You went to the h. . . .?").
- If your child still can't come up with the word, try offering choices (e.g., "Did you go to the hockey store or the hardware store?"). Analyzing other choices helps the brain pull the word more successfully the next time it looks for it. Using choices with similar initial sounds or similar meanings makes the task more productive.
- Make sure all the teachers who work with your child are acquainted with any special needs once they have been professionally identified. Unfortunately, not all teachers read their students' records and reports thoroughly.
- Keep an eye out for tests with low scores, particularly when you know your child studied and knew the material. Were the incorrect responses fill-in-the-blank formats?
- Make sure your child gets a word bank on tests, from which she can select the answers to fill in the blanks. Multiple-choice and

matching columns are other good alternatives. Have this modification written into the IEP so that it is legally binding. If this is not happening, talk to the teacher and speech-language pathologist. Then, if the teacher does not follow through on the IEP recommendations, speak to a school administrator.

- Teach your child new words in context or in phrases. Put each new word on a card in a meaningful sentence. Your son or daughter will associate the word with the sentence and therefore have some way to file the word (e.g., "Summer and winter are SEASONS" instead of using the word *seasons* on a blank index card or as part of a list of words).

- Help your child use mnemonic devices when studying for tests, whenever possible. To refresh your memory, a mnemonic device is when you try to find a "word" that can be made from the initial letters in any group. For example, you may still remember the names of the Great Lakes from your social studies class by the word HOMES, which represented lakes Huron, Ontario, Michigan, Erie, and Superior. When remembering a group of words, this strategy is invaluable.

- Help your child remember new words by putting them in songs. Remember that old song about the toe bone connected to the foot bone? Singing (or "rapping") the information allows the brain to make other associations in another part of the brain. Let the right side of the brain help the left side!

Case Study: Jay

Jay was in the fourth grade and getting by. He was consistently scoring in the C range on his social studies and science tests, but in other areas he was clearly an A or B student. His classroom teacher happened to eat lunch with me, and as Mrs. Jordan corrected her latest set of science tests (between bites of turkey sandwich), she sighed as she corrected Jay's paper. "He did so well when we discussed this in class the other day. I know he knows this. What happens to him when he takes these tests? Maybe he's just not a good test-taker or maybe he needs tutoring."

Of course, any professional connected with the special education field has antennae that go up anytime a student has "unexplained" difficulty, particularly when it seems inconsistent with the child's ability. And so, I began to examine Jay's test. All the multiple-choice questions were correct. In fact, the errors were primarily in the fill-in-the-blank sections, which were still, well . . . blank. So I began to ask some pointed questions, which led to a very interesting discussion.

Mrs. Jordan described how Jay punctuates his comments with an inordinate amount of hms *and* uhs, *taking forever to get out a simple statement. Even when the sentence comes out, the words Jay uses are often vague. For example, when the class was asked how they spent their Thanksgiving holiday, Jay was eager to respond. "We uh . . . drove to my Mom's friend's little house up there. It's a . . . brown one by that big thing-uh-monnoment-uh-mon-U-ment . . . over in the town. You know, the one with the big ski things in it? We really liked it!" When Mrs. Jordan asked specific questions about the trip, Jay was able to supply answers. He did understand where he went and what he did; he was simply unable to express it clearly with clear, concise language. He often puts himself down and sometimes mutters with frustration under his breath.*

After hearing this and speaking with Jay's mother (who was getting quite frazzled trying to help him pass these tests and figure out what he was trying to say at times), I pursued a formal speech-language and learning disability evaluation. The evaluation supported a diagnosis of a word retrieval deficit, with additional expressive language delays as well. Often children like Jay have other organizational and sequential problems that are consistent with a learning disability. Jay did show evidence of a mild learning disability.

Learning disabilities *are often defined as being a gap in a child's ability (which by legal definition is within the average range or higher) and his or her academic performance. To determine Jay's ability, a psychologist performed an IQ test, which supported our expectation that Jay was certainly not a "slow" child.*

Language therapy was recommended for Jay, but what helped him most were modifications in the classroom and an increased understanding on the part of his teachers and parents. I was able to discuss the diagnosis in simple terms with Jay, who was relieved to know he was not as "stupid" as he thought. The special education teacher provided assistance in the classroom and consulted with the classroom teacher to make sure the lessons, assignments, and tests were structured appropriately for Jay.

Jay continues to do well in school with modifications in the classroom and consultation between his teachers and parents.

The "I Don't Know How to Explain It" Child: Sequencing, Referential, and Divergent Language Problems

I know Tatiana is a bright girl. She gets straight As in math and is a whiz in art, music, and PE! I think that's because she likes those classes better. She just sits and stares at the paper for half the period during language arts. If I prod her, she'll put a few words down every once in a while, but it's like pulling teeth. If she had a learning disability, she wouldn't be such a good reader, right? So she must just be lazy, I guess.

—F. G., teacher

Some children, even those with average or above-average intellectual ability, don't know where to start to explain something. For them to tell a story or describe what happened yesterday is nothing short of a challenge. The inability to logically organize their thoughts affects what they say as well as what they write. Children with expressive language problems typically have difficulty with these types of tasks, even if their speech skills and grammar use are normal.

In this section, we cover more about the kinds of language use problems children exhibit, how these problems affect children, and what parents can do about them.

Sequencing Problems

Sequencing refers to putting things in the right order. Sequencing problems can take many forms. Some children have problems sequencing sounds, so that when they try to spell a word, they have difficulty figuring out which sounds to write down and in which order. When children have difficulty pronouncing long words, it is sometimes caused by a problem sequencing syllables. Some children have difficulty sequencing when trying to name the days of the week or months of the year.

Tatiana's sequencing problem involves putting words (language) into some kind of order so that there is a cohesive, logical flow from thought to thought. Children who exhibit sequencing problems when they speak may be at risk for having other sequencing problems that can interfere in their ability to perform successfully at school. These are often part of a larger constellation of organizational weaknesses related to a **language-learning disability.**

Tatiana is a very good reader. Her problem is more subtle, so it is easy to miss. She is excelling in the other subjects, such as art and math, because she doesn't need to do much writing or speaking in those classes.

Certainly most "normal" preschool children have difficulty with sequencing tasks. Even if they have seen a video 25 times in one week, it may be all but impossible to elicit any more than "the little boy was lost and they had a party and it was so funny!" As children reach first and second grade, the brain becomes more conscious of order. Left and right.

Beginning and ending. First, second, and third. Stories have plots with a beginning, middle, and end. It is when these concepts and tasks present a special challenge that a problem may become more and more apparent. This is one reason why this kind of problem is typically diagnosed at a later age.

A child with a language sequencing problem can tell you bits and pieces about a story, character, or favorite part but often cannot start from the beginning and tell you what happened in an organized or logical way, even at the age of ten. One of the reasons Tatiana may be hesitating to write a word on the paper during writing classes is because she doesn't know where the beginning of the story is. What should she say first?

Children with serious attention-span problems often have difficulty with sequencing tasks because they can't think about one thing long enough to get it organized. Their brains dart from subject to subject, never allowing enough time to put things in order.

Sometimes looking at pictures in the right order helps the child organize thoughts, but pictures are not always practical when you want your child to tell you about the incident on the playground at school today!

Sequencing problems present a special long-term challenge to children, as well as adults. As with many language problems, therapy can help your child improve these skills, but you should not expect a cure.

Referential Problems

"My sister and Mom went shopping Tuesday, but she didn't buy anything." *Who* didn't buy anything? From this sentence, it's hard to tell.

Referential skills help the listener know who or what you are talking about. A child with poor referential skills will use too many pronouns (*he, she, it, they,* etc.) and indefinite pronouns (*this, that,* etc.) when they speak. Referential skills are another component of expressive language that is important to a child's ability to communicate easily with other people. As with sequencing skills, referential skills are usually developed as a child reaches first and second grade. Weak referential skills are also sometimes one piece of a bigger language-learning disabled profile.

Referential skills can be improved with language therapy but may need to be worked into other language activities and developed in time.

Divergent Language Problems

"Tell me everything you can about this picture." For many children like Tatiana, this kind of open-ended task presents yet another set of problems. If I showed Tatiana the same picture and asked her to "tell me what this lady is doing," I'm sure she could answer me easily. Tasks that ask the child to speak about a general topic or thing, such as a picture, are called *divergent* language tasks. Tatiana may have difficulty "getting started" in these types of tasks. She may also have difficulty figuring out what's important about the picture. She may talk about peripheral details, such as a bird flying overhead and a blue car driving on the road, and may mention incidentally the raging fire that is the centerpoint of the picture.

Problems with **divergent language skills** show up when a child is asked to create a sentence with a particular word in it, a typical spelling homework assignment. What does the child say about it? The child may sit and think, stare out a window, write a word or two, and then get distracted with other thoughts.

When asked to write in a journal or about a topic such as snow, Tatiana would probably sit and turn over thoughts in her mind while the rest of the class is starting to work on editing their finished stories. However, if the teacher told her to write about a specific topic such as "what you like to do after school," Tatiana might have more success.

Characteristics of Children Who Have Problems Explaining

Children with sequencing, referential, or divergent language problems might:

- Have average or above-average intellectual ability
- Have learning disabilities in other areas, such as reading or perceptual problems
- Take an inordinate amount of time to get started with an answer to an open-ended question such as, "Tell me about plants."
- Jump around when retelling stories, put events out of any logical order, or leave out essential information
- Start and stop in midsentence, changing words as the sentences unfold such as, "He . . . uh . . . I mean she . . . uh, was going shopping, uh . . . well she had *gone* shopping, but it—I didn't know and uh . . . "
- Confuse *left/right* and *first/last*
- Think the listener is following the dialogue, when in fact the listener is confused
- Have difficulty staying on one task or paying attention
- Say "I don't know" rather than struggle to explain something

- Have difficulty answering essay questions
- Have difficulty writing stories with events in the correct order, although ideas may be creative
- Have difficulty putting months or days of the week in order
- Have difficulty initiating social conversations or thinking of things to say
- Possess much knowledge but have difficulty expressing it verbally and/or in writing
- Miss the "bigger picture" and focus on unimportant details
- Have word retrieval problems

How Do Problems Explaining Affect a Child?

Because children with expressive language problems often have difficulty "explaining," they may find "chit-chat" very draining. They feel awkward if their search for the right words causes lulls in their conversations. But if they start talking too quickly, the rambling and "starts and stops" can leave listeners in the dust and the children feeling even more anxious.

In school, an expressive language problem is most likely to affect a child during classroom discussions and when writing essays. When asked to do a report, children like Tatiana will need help getting started and organized. Remember, the problems these children have when trying to explain verbally usually present a problem when writing. They may need to be told very specifically what information should be answered in a report.

These children may be able to answer direct questions quite well, particularly if the teacher is looking for a one-word answer, but they will likely struggle when it comes to answering essay questions and writing book reports.

There are several reasons for this phenomenon. Developing paragraphs and an outline requires an organized mind. To come up with ideas, you must be able to draw associations and recall information you already know and put it down on paper. The same organization and expressive language ability is required to give speeches or explain the results of a group science project. If these areas are delayed in your child, school may become increasingly tedious and overwhelming as time goes on. Your son or daughter knows the information, but explaining it or putting it down on paper is torturous.

At home, parents will probably need to ask several questions to find out the answers to questions such as "What happened at school today?" A child like Tatiana may answer with a one-word response, such as

"Nothing." Putting thoughts together, figuring out where to start, and thinking of what words to use can be exhausting, particularly after a long day at school! On other days, such a child may respond with a confusing answer such as "OK, I just wish he didn't put the answers on the board until I was done. Yesterday it was only five minutes!" You may be able to piece together what happened, but the way it is expressed is confusing.

Socially, a child like Tatiana may be able to float along, without a huge impact on her ability to form and keep friendships. In my experience, most other children seem to be patient about drawing children like Tatiana out or asking questions to clarify something that confuses them. Tatiana may be perceived as a shy or quiet child. In fact, she may gravitate toward sports or the arts, where communication is more nonverbal, such as painting or drawing, music, or dance.

Your child may have difficulty in classes that require lots of report writing or oral reports. Using outlines and notecards will help, but chances are he will have more success in other kinds of classes such as science labs, computers, math, arts, mechanics, woodworking, or other hands-on classes. The areas in which your son or daughter finds success in school will also likely affect the career he or she chooses.

Therapy for a Child Who Has Problems Explaining

Therapy to address problems with explaining rarely "cures" the child of the problem, although it can certainly improve it. Sometimes, a child's naturally shy personality or learning disability make it difficult to significantly change what is essentially a weak style of communicating.

In therapy, the child will start by learning how to explain very short pieces of information or stories. Gradually the length and complexity of the task is increased. The focus may be on using descriptive words and phrases, retelling events or stories in order (sequencing), or simply knowing how to get started and mentally organized when asked an open-ended question. If the child's area of difficulty is referential skills, learning how to be specific and avoid vague language will be important. Typically, a child with weak expressive language skills will need to focus on nearly all these tasks to some degree.

Some speech-language pathologists also spend time helping the child to improve these skills in written language as well as oral language. Since reports and essays require organization and elaboration of language, they lend themselves well to language intervention, especially at the upper primary and middle school grades.

What Can Parents Do to Help a Child Who Has Problems with Explaining?

If you suspect your child has a problem like Tatiana's, seek a professional's opinion. If your child has already been diagnosed with an expressive language problem of this type, here are some ways you can help:

- Be patient. Give your child extra time to respond verbally. Time pressure is apt to make her grab at verbal straws and become anxious.
- Avoid open-ended oral questions such as, "Tell me about your ballgame." Instead, ask specific questions such as, "Did your teammates make any exciting plays today?"
- After watching movies, TV shows, or videos, help your child to reconstruct the essential elements of the story. Draw pictures of important scenes together and help put them in order. Write captions under the pictures.
- Use family photographs to help your child talk about things that have happened. Try to take several pictures over the course of an event so your child can later put them in order and retell the event. Later, see if she can tell someone else about the event without looking at the pictures.
- Help your child with independent open-ended projects, such as "Write a report about Paul Revere." Find out what information the teacher wants. Help your child develop an outline before she attempts to tackle the assignment and show how to take it one step at a time. Otherwise, your child will be overwhelmed with everything at once. For example, the Paul Revere assignment could be broken into four parts: (1) Write about Paul Revere's childhood; (2) write about what he did before the Revolutionary War; (3) describe what happened during the war; and (4) tell about what he did after the war and when he died.
- Look at your child's tests. If she is struggling with essay questions on tests, you may need to talk to the speech-language pathologist to discuss whether your child can be tested in another, more appropriate way.

As a parent, you may need to help your child with these kinds of homework assignments on a regular basis or face hours of a nonproductive tug-of-war between you. Sometimes it helps just knowing your child isn't being lazy but has a specific kind of language disorder or deficit. You'll know you can't expect your child to excel at these types of activities any more than a clumsy child can be expected to excel at the balance beam. Understanding the situation can perhaps ease the guilt of feeling like you're "helping too much." A professional can guide you as to the best strategy for helping your child, who is apt to have unique needs.

Case Study: Jackson

Ten-year-old Jackson was well liked by his teachers and peers, but it was clear he was having some problems. When he was 8 years old and in the second grade, Jackson had been diagnosed with perceptual problems, *which are a type of learning disability. These perceptual problems had become apparent when he had difficulty learning to read and spell. His handwriting was often "sloppy" and poorly spaced on a page. In fact, his desk was a mess, and his room at home was in equal disarray. Jackson was what we sometimes call a "loose" kid; he was a little unravelled, but, oh, so lovable. Things got lost and assigments were frequently misplaced or accidentally forgotten. He received extra help through the resource room in school and a special reading program.*

What wasn't apparent in the second grade, though, was that Jackson also had problems with expressive language. As he grew older, in addition to having the perceptual problem of putting sounds in order, it became clear that Jackson was having problems putting words and sentences in order as well. When Jackson was in second grade, his teachers and parents had recognized the trouble Jackson had with explaining things, but this was less of a concern at that time than his below-average reading and writing skills. His expressive language problems seemed minor in comparison to his other problems, so speech-language testing was not discussed at this time.

As Jackson's spelling and reading improved, he was expected to write longer stories with greater detail and a coherent plot. In class, discussions became more philosophical and abstract. Projects were assigned with fewer "restrictions" and greater room for creativity. Unfortunately, the "room for creativity" was too much room for a child like Jackson. Getting started was so difficult for him that he just didn't start at all.

Jackson's fifth-grade classroom teacher referred his case to the Child Study Team. She was looking for behavioral strategies to motivate him to complete these projects. His mother was also at her wit's end with him, with each project becoming a nightly battleground. Jackson was also less willing to take part in classroom discussions than he used to be. He was scoring in the B-C range on tests unless an essay question was asked. He usually bombed on those.

Since Jackson was already identified as a special education student, various motivational strategies were discussed by the team. Perhaps he would do better on the tests if he studied more? Did he need more time to do the projects? Were they too difficult? I asked Jackson's parents for permission to perform a thorough speech and language evaluation to assess Jackson's higher-level language skills to see whether there was another reason for these problems.

On the language battery, Jackson excelled on the vocabulary subtests and language-processing tasks. However, when he was asked to describe a very busy picture or a construction scene, there was a pause for about a minute. He squirmed in his seat and nervously tapped a pencil.

"Well, uh . . . which thing do you want me to tell you about?"

"Tell me everything you can about the picture," I replied.

"Oh . . . uh . . . it's got that—I mean it looks like it's sorta a . . . a . . . guy laying bricks and the cat is looking into the house. Well—it's not really a house yet; the guys are building the house . . . I mean they are going to build a house. Oh, forget it. I don't know."

When asked him to tell the story of his favorite movie, this is what he told me: ". . . Uh . . . well, I don't know. Yeah, I've seen it about a hundred times, but um . . . it's hard to explain . . . It's about a guy who does a lot of . . . has a lot of adventures. When he was almost killed, the big boulder almost fell on top of him and it really was radical . . . really radical. But first he was at his father's ranch for a while. The girl in the movie—Johanna—she took—uh . . . I mean she wanted to . . . hmm . . . Well they both really wanted to find a secret cave. But the guy that had—uh . . . that rock was so big, really . . . it was so radical."

Did you catch that? You are probably a bit confused and still know very little about the plot to the movie. If you asked Jackson something specific about that movie, he could tell you. It's not that he forgets, it's just that it all gets so scrambled up in his mind that it comes out wrong.

Jackson was diagnosed as having an expressive language disorder. With his other learning disabilities, he could also be called language-learning disabled. These disorders are typically interrelated. The missing piece to Jackson's earlier diagnosis had been his sequencing and organizational language problems. He also exhibited word retrieval problems.

Once his teachers and parents understood the obstacles Jackson faced, assignments and tests were tailored to help compensate and develop the appropriate skills. He was enrolled in weekly group "speech" therapy sessions (as I mentioned earlier, this therapy has more to do with language than speech), which helped him develop strategies to compensate for his deficits.

Jackson will probably always have difficulty getting organized. Nar-

rative writing and explaining and describing will probably never be his strong suits, either. But with increased understanding and the development of these language skills, Jackson can handle school with far less anxiety and negative impact on his self-esteem, and he will receive the help he needs to develop these much needed skills.

7

Understanding Listening Problems

As we've discussed earlier, language is both receptive and expressive. Since receptive language refers to how well we comprehend language, a listening problem can be the root of a receptive language weakness. After all, if information is not getting heard as it was intended, it will be difficult to comprehend. In many cases, the term *receptive language deficit* is used interchangeably with *language processing deficit* or even *auditory processing deficit.* Much research stills needs to be done in this area. Sometimes it is difficult to tell whether a child is having difficulty comprehending what people say because the ears are not processing sounds correctly or the brain is not processing what the ears are sending. Some tests are available to help answer this question, but it is not always possible to tell whether the child has a processing or a comprehension problem.

In this chapter I describe the difficulties faced by children with common listening problems. I discuss central auditory processing disorders, in which children struggle to distinguish speech from background noise; auditory memory problems, where children forget much of what they hear; and language processing problems, in which children have difficulty comprehending what is said to them. As always, I explain how these conditions affect the children at school and home, and I detail what parents can do to help them cope.

The "What? Did You Say Something?" Child: A Central Auditory Processing Problem

Eddie is a very bright boy, but sometimes I just don't understand what is wrong with him. I know he hears me because we've had his hearing checked by several people. But sometimes I call his name and he never looks up. When I call on him, I usually have to repeat the question because he's been daydreaming or tuning me out. He also doesn't pay attention to the other children during class discussions and is distracted by every little noise in the hall or outside. When I work with him one-to-one, he does much better, but I don't have the time to do this with 25 children in my classroom. What can I do?

—Miss Donnelly, 2nd grade teacher

Children like Eddie are a real puzzle. Parents and teachers *know* they are bright, yet something is not quite right. Although it's true that a very creative and gifted child can respond to being bored in school by daydreaming, many children have a weakness that prevents them from listening in a normal way. It is out of their control.

When a child is of preschool age, you expect listening to be a challenge, particularly when the child is required to sit for long periods of time. A problem like Eddie's may go unnoticed until second grade or even later, because so often it seems like something the child will grow out of or that it is just a matter of controlling the child's behavior.

In this section, we'll look at ways to recognize and understand children with Eddie's problem and examine what can be done for them.

One cause of Eddie's problem may be a *central auditory processing disorder.* Having a central auditory processing disorder means that Eddie's ears are able to hear sounds, but his brain perceives the sounds in a different way than a typical person does. This causes problems for a child when listening because it takes a great deal of concentration and effort to comprehend what people say. Words may sound "mumbly," so sometimes the child may misinterpret what is said or ask "What?" often. In a noisy setting, focusing on one voice is physically difficult; for example, when a door is being opened or closed or feet are shuffling, it is distracting. Since listening requires so much effort for them, these children tend to get "tired of listening" much more quickly than a typical child. The daydreamer or doodler may need a break from concentrated listening.

Children with central auditory processing disorders may go undiagnosed for many reasons. For one, people often assume if a child can hear a beeping noise on a hearing test, that child should be able to listen normally. Hearing sounds and listening, however, are two different tasks. Listening to speech requires much more than knowing a sound is being made. It requires the child to hear the difference between *hear* and *hair, three* and *free.* Hearing differences between similar words and sounds is called *auditory discrimination* or **speech discrimination.** Children with a central auditory processing disorder may have problems hearing those subtle differences in words. This can also cause a problem when a child spells words, because he needs to know which sounds come in which order in a word to write it down.

Children with a central auditory processing disorder may be learning to spell and read by memorizing words, rather than sounding them out. For example, a child may sound out a word, such as *c-a-t,* then say *couch* or *candle* or *tack* or any other similar word. These children do this because they forget the sounds by the time the last letter is pronounced. This is called an **auditory sequencing** problem. It is a type of auditory processing disorder and is often a problem for children with central auditory processing problems.

Another reason these children go undiagnosed is because they perform so much better in a quiet room, which is where a specialist will tend to perform the initial speech or language testing. Thus, in that environment, children may follow directions, pay attention, and "listen" very well, scoring at or above their age level. Yet, in a classroom or at a lively dinner table discussion, they are clearly confused sometimes, misinterpreting what is said, needing it repeated, and forgetting what was said. Why the difference? The nature of a central auditory processing disorder is that the child's ability to listen is greatly influenced by what is going on around him and how the voice is heard. In a gymnasium, on the telephone, in a cafeteria, or through a speaker in a classroom, voices are acoustically somewhat different. Children with central auditory processing disorders have difficulty listening to speech in these settings. In addition to being distracted by even the slightest noise, another very real problem for these children is that a person's voice is acoustically more challenging to process with other noise present.

Children also may go undiagnosed because central auditory processing disorders have only been discussed in-depth in professional literature and research in the past five or ten years. Facilities for testing are not widely available, and there has been some professional debate as to the validity of the diagnosis and treatment. Many speech-language pathologists, pediatricians, and other professionals are still learning what a central auditory processing disorder is all about. However, as time goes on, it is becoming increasingly commonplace to refer those children who exhibit problems listening for this type of testing, particularly when the problem has no other explanation. Unlike children with Attention Deficit Disorder, children with central auditory processing disorders are able to stay on a task (such as completing a worksheet) if it does not involve listening. They are not, as a rule, impulsive in their behavior and are not distracted by movement or colorful objects any more than an average child. They also don't have difficulty staying on one topic the way a child with Attention Deficit Disorder does or have trouble telling a story in order. These are just a few of the differences between these two conditions.

Studies by Tallal (1976) and Sloan (1986) show that there is a relationship between children who have speech and language problems and those who have central auditory processing disorders. Although much research needs to be done in this area, there seems to be evidence to suggest that some children with central auditory processing disorders speak differently because they are trying to imitate the words in the mumbly way in which they hear them. (This is another reason why this book addresses all three areas of speech, language, and listening. The three are very closely interdependent and interrelated.)

There is also research (Keith, 1981) that suggests a relationship between children who have had frequent middle ear infections (*otitis media*) and the presence of central auditory processing disorders. This is true even if the child is no longer experiencing the infections or fluid. As discussed in chapter 2, children with a history of frequent ear infections are also at risk for developing other speech and language problems. Since children with speech and language problems are at risk for developing a central auditory processing disorder, this is one more way speech, language, and listening skills are connected.

Central auditory processing disorders are diagnosed by an audiologist, although a speech-language pathologist or other professional or parent may make the referral for the testing. The evaluation takes place in a soundproof room specially equipped to accommodate this kind of testing. Headphones are placed on the child's ears, and she is asked to perform various listening tasks, such as repeating words and sentences heard in the headphones. The child is presented words and sentences in different ways, with noise in the background. At this time, you may find only a handful of places in your state that do this kind of testing due to both the expense of the setup and the relative newness of our knowledge about this disorder. Your child's speech-language pathologist or ear-nose-throat physician can help you find someone who does this testing. You may have to go to a university or city to have this testing done.

Characteristics of Children with a Central Auditory Processing Disorder

Children who have a central auditory processing disorder may exhibit a variety of behaviors. Remember, however, that a diagnosis is made based on the results of audiological tests, not on the basis of observation of these behaviors. Children with central auditory processing disorders might do the following:

- Have difficulty staying focused on what someone is saying when there is noise or other distractions in the background
- Have difficulty listening for long periods of time
- Confuse or forget what people say
- Say "Huh?" or "What?" frequently
- Not turn around or react when someone calls their name
- Be easily distracted when listening
- Have difficulty sounding out words when learning to read
- Have difficulty spelling words
- Exhibit speech problems
- Exhibit problems learning new words
- Exhibit difficulty with reading comprehension

How Does a Central Auditory Processing Problem Affect a Child?

At home, you might find it difficult to get your child's attention if she is in the next room, especially if the TV or washing machine is on. Once you do get her attention, it may be difficult to keep for more than a minute or two. If a radio is playing in the background or siblings are running around playing, you may find it impossible to have a meaningful conversation.

Due to acoustical conditions, having a conversation in the car or on the phone may also be a very difficult task, particularly if a radio is playing in the background. If your child plays on a sports team or attends noisy club meetings, she may seem "lost" or "tuned out" at times. These situations present a special challenge for a child with a central auditory processing disorder. People's voices are competing with each other, and in a large room or outdoor area, the acoustics make it difficult for the child to hear clearly.

School is probably the place where a central auditory processing disorder affects a child the most because of the intensity of the listening required, the amount of time listening is required, and the number of distractions present. And because of the relationship between central auditory processing disorders and speech, reading (sounding out words), and writing, a child may need extra help in those academic areas as well. However, a central auditory disorder need not be a permanent or debilitating problem and can be managed in a way that your child can function successfully at school with the right help.

Children with this problem may also have difficulty comprehending what they read as well as what they hear. However, when reading, the child can go back and reread the passage over and over until it has "sunk in." With listening, there is no way to recapture the words unless they are written down. These problems may be significant enough to warrant a special education label of "learning disabled" in school.

Children with a central auditory processing disorder may have problems keeping up their grades, particularly if a teacher teaches primarily by lecturing. This is especially true for classes like social studies and science. Thus, it is important to properly diagnose this problem so accommodations can be made for the child in the classroom. The audiologist, speech-language pathologist, and learning disabilities teacher should work together to adjust classroom lessons so your child can learn successfully.

Children with a central auditory processing problem may seem to ignore the teacher, daydreaming as Eddie does. They may watch the other children to make sure they are following the directions correctly. This copying behavior may be easily misinterpreted by the teacher.

However, with therapy and understanding, these children can function successfully in the classroom and at home.

Therapy for Central Auditory Processing Disorders

Testing and diagnosing this problem has become more common in recent years, but treatment programs are still being developed to address the problem. Most audiologists prefer to wait until a child is 7 or older before making a firm diagnosis in order to give the child's system time to mature. To help a child with this disorder experience success at school, it is critical to make the classroom as quiet as possible. Sometimes having carpeting on the floor and making other acoustical improvements can make a big difference. For the most part, a teacher should treat the child as though he *does* have a hearing problem, because most of the recommendations are appropriate for a child with a hearing impairment and that is how the child is functioning. For example, the child should sit close to the teacher, who should speak slowly and simply while facing the child. Writing directions and key pieces of information on the black-board helps. Repeating and rephrasing important information may be necessary.

Therapy can be provided by an audiologist or a speech-language pathologist. If it is to be handled by the speech pathologist, the audiologist who makes the diagnosis should guide that speech pathologist as to the kind of therapy that will help the child most.

A device called an **FM system** (also called an **auditory trainer**) can be particularly useful for a child with a pronounced central auditory processing problem. To use an FM system, the teacher attaches a mini-microphone, which receives the teacher's voice, to a clip worn on the collar. This is wired to a small transmitter that can be clipped to a belt or the top of a pair of pants. The student wears headphones, a loop, or other device, which is wired to a receiver that is clipped to a belt, a harness, or the top of a pair of pants also. This technology allows the child to hear the teacher's voice with far less distraction, although other children's voices can still be heard. It helps the child stay better focused on what the teacher is saying, and the child doesn't tire as quickly from listening.

I have worked with a few children who have retested in the "normal" range on these tests and no longer displayed any observable listening weaknesses after receiving therapy for a year or two. (These particular children, however, did not have any other speech, language, or learning weaknesses.) But for many, if not most, children, a central auditory processing problem is only one piece of a bigger learning disability; therefore, they may always struggle in some way with listening tasks.

What Can Parents Do to Help a Child with a Central Auditory Processing Problem?

If your child has been diagnosed with a central auditory processing disorder, the audiologist who diagnosed the problem has probably given you plenty of practical tips. If he or she hasn't, ask. This is particularly necessary because each child is different and, depending on the results of the evaluation, may have special needs. The following are some general suggestions that are somewhat universal for children with central auditory processing problems:

- Don't try to have a conversation if your child is in another room. Walk directly to where your child is before speaking.
- Make sure your child is looking at you and ready to listen before beginning a conversation.

- Reduce the noise level in your home when having a family discussion or conversation. Go into a quiet room, turn off the TV, or close a door if needed.
- If your home is noisy due to tile or hardwood floors, consider carpeting your living areas. This flooring will improve the acoustics and make it easier for your child to hear.
- If you find yourself in a noisy situation, speak just a little more loudly. This will help your child focus on your voice and tune out the background noise, which is difficult to filter out.
- Speak slowly and pause between thoughts. This gives your child time to process what you say.
- Repeat and rephrase important messages. If your child can read, write them down in a conspicuous place.

Case Study: Ramon

Mrs. Edelman, Ramon's third-grade teacher, stopped me in the teacher's room one day. She was wondering what to do with Ramon. She was sure he had a hearing problem, especially since he still had tubes in his ears as a result of past ear infections. But the school nurse double-checked his hearing and assured Mrs. Edelman it was normal. Now what could she do? Ramon didn't seem to hear her much of the time. When she called on him, he didn't know what was going on or answered a related question but not the one she asked. He frequently said "What?"

The teacher told me Ramon's reading was in the low-average range—just low enough that he was struggling, but not enough for him to qualify for special education services. He seemed to be a bright boy but frequently copied other children's work. She guessed that he must not be paying attention. Mrs. Edelman knew that something was not quite right, but since Ramon was not failing, she was hesitant to push for testing. "What should I do?" she asked me.

I observed Ramon informally in class on several occasions. When he paid attention, he seemed to keep up with the rest of the class, but his attention was usually fleeting. Mrs. Edelman continually had to prompt him to look at her. He was seated near the open window, where he could hear a lawnmower humming throughout the lesson, and he looked out the window frequently.

When I spoke with Ramon's mother, she expressed exasperation with him at home. "He doesn't listen," she said. "I ask him to do something and it's like it goes in one ear and out the other! For instance, if I ask him to go upstairs and brush his teeth, get on his pajamas, and pick out a book to read, I can go upstairs in 20 minutes and find him sitting there, fully clothed, reading a book."

Ramon's mother and teacher filled out a referral form for our school's Child Study Team and requested testing to find out the source of Ramon's problems. The learning disabilities teacher did an evaluation and found Ramon had some strong skills in many academic areas, especially math and spelling. However, it was noted that Ramon was memorizing most of the words he knew how to read and spell because he was unable to figure out how to read or spell made-up words, such as fip or tibe. He had no idea how to go about sounding them out or spelling them. Since Ramon was not failing in reading or spelling, his problem had easily escaped notice.

He also needed to have the test questions repeated often, because he misunderstood what the evaluator said. He needed frequent breaks from the testing because he became easily "overloaded" from all the questions and concentration.

On the speech-language evaluation, Ramon scored very high on the vocabulary tests and even did well on most of the language and listening tests. (It is not uncommon for children with central auditory processing disorders to do well on listening tasks in a quiet environment or for short periods of time.) The tests that did give him trouble were the tasks that asked him to listen to sounds such as t-oa-s-t or syllables such as el-e-va-tor and figure out what the word was. These tasks, along with those that tested his ability to remember a series of words or long sentences, were below average. However, overall Ramon's testing was not low enough to qualify for a special education classification.

With his parents' permission, our team referred Ramon to an audiologist for a central auditory processing evaluation. The testing showed a clear-cut, significant central auditory processing disorder. Ramon was unable to perceive speech clearly with even a minimal amount of background noise or when part of the message was missing. Thus, he now qualified for a special education program, which allowed us to tailor an individual program for him, combining therapy with changes in the way the classroom teacher presented lessons and tests.

The audiologist asked us to try an FM listening system to help keep Ramon focused on the teacher's voice. We also moved his seat so he was close to the teacher and away from the window. The teacher was asked to write directions on the blackboard and speak more slowly. Other suggestions for teaching strategies were included on the child's IEP. (See chapter 4 for a full explanation of the IEP.)

At home, Ramon's mother and father realized they would need to be patient with him. They no longer tried to give him long directions or have *conversations in the kitchen while the dishwasher was running. When they needed to get his attention, they waited until he was looking at them before talking. In the car, they turned off the radio and spoke slowly and clearly so that Ramon could focus on their voices. On the soccer field and basketball court, they helped his coaches understand how difficult it was for Ramon to follow a coach's voice from 20 feet away. His coaches agreed to pull Ramon closer to help him comprehend what they were saying. These and other suggestions have helped Ramon's family cope very well with his weaknesses in auditory processing.*

Ramon is now in eighth grade. He no longer needs any direct therapy services for his central auditory processing disorder. In fact, tests show his problem is now clinically "mild." He is still classified as a special education student, however, because teachers still need to meet with the SLP from time to time to review his progress and ways they can modify their instructional methods to accommodate his needs. If the school had an audiologist on staff, he or she would be the primary specialist involved with Ramon's program. However, since Ramon's school, like most public schools, does not have one, Ramon is tested each year by an audiologist with whom the district contracts for this service. Ramon resisted wearing the FM system after a year or two, so it was phased out. Ramon is pulling As in math, science, art, PE, and social studies with no help, although he needs to take careful notes and study with diligence. He works very hard for his grades. Language arts are still difficult for Ramon. His spelling and reading skills are weak but in the C+ range.

The "I Forgot What You Said" Child: An Auditory Memory Problem

Yesterday Mrs. Sauer was telling us what to do, and I couldn't remember what she said, so I asked Jamaal 'cause he's smart. When she caught me askin' him, she got really mad because she said I should pay attention better, but the words just fly out of my head like a bird.

—Tamina, age 5

Do you know a child like Tamina? A child who looks right at you and seems to be listening but can't remember what you said? Maybe you can relate to Tamina's mother. She's at the end of her rope this morning. Is Tamina ignoring her, or has she truly forgotten to go upstairs, brush her hair, and bring down her spelling book? What exactly *is* she doing up there?! Tamina's mother gets so exasperated . . . especially after repeating those directions for the second and third time in ten minutes. Is Tamina deliberately trying to test her patience?

In this section, I discuss a kind of listening problem Tamina is exhibiting, how it affects children, and what parents can do about it.

Interestingly, Tamina is a crackerjack when it comes to remembering where pieces of a puzzle go or how to get to her aunt's house. If she can remember those things, then why can't she remember what people say?

The brain doesn't have one specific place for memory. In fact, there are many kinds of memories stored in different places and ways by the brain. You can remember smells, tastes, emotions, songs, events, and what your mother looked like as she tucked you in. These are just a few kinds of information stored by our brain. Once the information is stored, it becomes part of our memory.

When children like Tamina have difficulty remembering what people say, it is not because they can't hear the words or understand the message. It is because their brain cannot hold on to the words long enough for them to make sense of the message. The word *auditory* refers to the way we hear and interpret sounds and words. Tamina has an *auditory memory deficit.* It is a common type of listening disorder that can seriously impact a child's ability to succeed in school. It can also cause enormous frustration for the parents!

Auditory memory develops in a child from a young age. It is a gradual process that requires intact hearing acuity, attention span, and remembering during the course of a typical day. Simple activities such as listening to stories read aloud, talking with a parent, and following along with songs and rhymes help a child develop auditory skills. Even with the best hearing and stimulation, however, a child may for many reasons still have an auditory memory problem.

If Tamina has difficulty keeping her attention on what is being said and is easily distracted, it will be even more difficult for her to remember verbal information. Therefore, attention span problems will also impact or cause an auditory memory problem. Medication may help children with Attention Deficit Disorder, a type of attention span problem, to stay focused longer, thus improving auditory memory skills.

Auditory memory problems are often not detected until a child is in school or given a thorough speech-language evaluation for other problems, such as speech delays or language weaknesses. Unlike speech problems, listening disorders are often not the kind of deficits that jump out at you if you are not looking for them. It is easy to assume the child is willfully disobeying the parent or teacher or just not paying attention.

To give you an idea of what it would feel like to have an auditory memory problem, read these directions quickly out loud: *Draw a large purple and red flower above the green door, but first underline each word with a* p *or* f *in it; cross out the second large triangle to the right of the small blue circle.* Now close your eyes and see how much of that you can remember. Did you remember it accurately? Chances are you remembered something about some shapes and a flower, maybe the letter *p.* But if you are like most people, the information was not stored. Reading the information also allowed you to see the words. When a child hears it only, the words linger in the air. There is not even a printed word to remember.

While you were reading those directions, you certainly understood each one individually, right? But when they were put together and spoken quickly, your brain could not hold on to them. When a child has an auditory memory problem, the same thing happens, except only a small amount of verbal information is needed to produce the same confusing effect.

Children with learning disabilities, short attention spans, speech and language problems, and other kinds of listening problems often have auditory memory deficits. This problem can be diagnosed with any number of tests given by a psychologist, learning disabilities specialist, audiologist, or speech-language pathologist. A typical way to test for an auditory memory problem is to say a sentence and ask the child to repeat it. As the sentences presented get longer and longer, the child not only may have difficulty remembering the exact wording but also typically may forget the *entire* thing once it gets too long. Another way to test auditory memory is to ask the child to respond to directions, which also get longer and more complex as the test progresses. A child whose only problem is a weak auditory memory will get the directions correct nearly all the time, if you repeat them several times without any further explanation. However, if you say them once or very quickly, the child may get only part of the direction correct or just say "I forget what to do."

For preschool children, auditory memory delays are also evident when you ask them to say *under the table* and they can only repeat *table.* A child with a delayed auditory memory may also have problems learning how to speak in full sentences or use new words because she can't remember the words to say.

A child who doesn't understand the directions or gets confused no matter how many times you say the directions has auditory (or language) *processing* problems. These are discussed later in this chapter.

Characteristics of Children with an Auditory Memory Problem

Children with an auditory memory problem might do the following:

- Have difficulty remembering oral directions, details of a story heard, or characters' names
- Watch what other children do before attempting to follow a verbal direction
- Remember only some parts of the direction, usually the last thing that was said
- Have a past history of frequent ear infections as an infant or toddler
- Have difficulty listening to lectures or discussions for long periods of time; may tune out after a while
- Have difficulty repeating back a multistep direction verbatim
- Have difficulty taking notes during class lectures; say the teacher "goes too fast"
- Have difficulty taking tests given orally
- Forget new words or concepts heard during a class lecture or need repetition and drills for them to "stick"
- Stumble over multisyllabic words; mix up syllables or mangle words when saying or writing them
- Learn more easily when watching what others are doing or use a hands-on approach
- Need to reread written information several times for it to "sink in"
- Have difficulty paying attention
- Forget new names easily
- Have difficulty memorizing their phone number, address, words to songs, poems, prayers, math facts

How Does an Auditory Memory Problem Affect a Child?

A child with an auditory memory problem is going to be at some disadvantage at home, but unfortunately the weakness will be more pronounced at school. Therefore, in the absence of other speech, language, or learning problems, an auditory memory deficit may not become noticeable until a child is 6, 7, or 8 years old. Delay in diagnosis is especially likely if the problem is mild.

Tamina's mother may remind her she wants to leave for Grandma's house after lunch, only to find Tamina's left to go play before her mother has even finished washing the lunch dishes. It's not that Tamina is trying to be difficult, it's just that she forgot what her mother told her. If her mother asked her, "Where are we supposed to go after lunch?" it may have jogged her memory or perhaps not. Tamina may remember hearing about going to Grandma's, but the "after lunch" part may have escaped her.

Learning the words to songs and nursery rhymes is difficult for pre-school children with auditory memory problems. This may cause frustration or embarrassment at times, but in my experience, children of this age seem generally unaware of this kind of problem. As children enter kindergarten, learning letter names and sounds may be difficult because these are primarily auditory memory tasks. If they can make associations (*A* is the letter in sister Ashley's name), they may remember it better.

It is a challenge for a child with an auditory memory problem to listen to a story and remember it the way other children do. As Tamina listens, she may comprehend what is being said, particularly if the sentences are simple and short. Unfortunately, as the sentences grow longer and more complex, the words become a mental blur. When the story is over, she may have trouble remembering any new words that were introduced, the characters' names, or other details related to the story.

In early grades, where learning is more hands-on, children often work together in groups, so if a child forgets the directions, it is easy for that child to watch what the others are doing. For these reasons, a child with an auditory memory problem may compensate for the weakness for some time, although reading and other language skills may be a challenge.

As stories, characters, and plots become more complex and filled with more details, there is more to remember, and the child will find it increasingly difficult to follow along. New words and concepts are discussed and taught at a quicker pace. Directions for worksheets and projects explained by the teacher grow more complex. A child with an auditory memory problem may begin to really fall apart in the second grade, particularly in the last half of the year. If the child is a strong reader, he can read back written directions several times or study the stories at home to help the information sink in. Although this strength helps the child compensate for a few years, it is exhausting for the child and the parent who has to spend so much extra time to help keep him going in school. The child may come home cranky and worn out and especially resistant to doing even more work at home.

Therapy for Children with Auditory Memory Problem

The classroom teacher may need to work with the specialists to present new information, directions, and stories in a different way (or give less of it) so your child is not too overwhelmed. These modifications should be included on your child's IEP (see chapter 4).

There are many ways a therapist or teacher can help children improve their ability to listen and remember what they hear. Often the focus is on teaching the child to use visualization or subvocalization to aid in memory. The specialist may teach the child how to take notes in a way to remember key points from a classroom discussion. Additional emphasis may be placed on teaching good listening behaviors such as maintaining eye contact with the teacher, keeping the body still, and requesting clarification when confused.

At this time, there is a lack of research proving the value of traditional listening "drills" that require a child to remember a series of words, numbers, sentences, or directions of increasing length. My experience shows that, without teaching the child how to do it better, this kind of practicing has little benefit.

What Can Parents Do to Help a Child with an Auditory Memory Problem?

If your child has been diagnosed with an auditory memory problem, you will need to be careful about the way you speak to your child. Try to do the following:

- Get your child's full attention and eye contact before continuing to speak ("Tamina, look at me. I want to tell you something.")
- Make sure you are in a quiet place when having a conversation. Turn off the TV, radio, dishwasher, and so forth.
- Remind your child to keep from touching or handling objects while listening (no tapping pencils, doodling, etc.).
- Keep your words short. Avoid long directions or complex sentences when speaking.
- Speak slowly and pause between thoughts.
- Give one direction at a time; wait until it is completed to give the next one.
- If your child can read, write down the directions so she can refer to them as needed. Numbering them in order helps (e.g., (1)

Make your bed, (2) put away your toys, and (3) brush your teeth).

Children with auditory memory deficits need after-school time to relax, play, and participate in activities that are not so frustrating and challenging. It may help a child's self-esteem to get involved in sports, learn a musical instrument, take up dance, or try any other "nonschool" activity. But there lies the dilemma: How do you help the child keep up with the class unless you spend considerable after-school time going over what was missed the first time in class?

Most schools set approximate time frames for children to spend at home each night on homework, depending on the grade level. Try to stick to the recommended time frame. If your child needs a great deal more time to keep up with the class, speak to your child's special education teacher or speech-language pathologist about it.

Case Study: Sarah

Sarah first came to my attention in November of her first-grade year. She was having some difficulty learning to read and spell, so her classroom teacher referred her to our Child Study Team for help. She also had difficulty following directions as well as grasping her pencil the right way when writing, so her printing was a bit sloppy. Since Sarah was one of the youngest children in her class and had no preschool experience, the team decided to take a conservative approach. She was given remedial reading help three times a week. The classroom teacher was given some strategies to try in the classroom to help Sarah learn her letters and sounds. For example, Sarah was given clay to squeeze to help her strengthen her fingers so she could grip her pencil better, and she used a larger pencil with a special rubber grip. The teacher tried to give class directions in a simpler way, demonstrating what to do when possible. Sarah's progress was monitored every few weeks for several months.

Sarah's mother was concerned at this point. Her husband had a learning disability as a child and remembered having problems from the very beginning, as Sarah was now experiencing. Her parents were anxious to prevent Sarah from getting too frustrated or feeling bad about herself. They worked with Sarah at home daily to help her learn her letters and spelling words.

By January, Sarah was doing better with her reading and spelling skills. She wasn't setting the world on fire, but she was making slow, steady progress. She still seemed lost at times when given directions, but she sat near a very patient little boy who would help her, so she was able to keep up in class. *The classroom teacher also tried to check on her frequently to make sure Sarah understood what she was supposed to do.*

At the end of the year, we discussed retaining Sarah in the first grade, but it was felt that Sarah would suffer more harm to her self-esteem by being retained than possibly struggling in second grade. Besides, she had already made friends with several children and was on the tall side, so the decision to place her in second grade was made.

In second grade, Sarah was quiet in class and rarely volunteered to answer questions. Her reading and spelling skills were marginal. She usually seemed to be paying attention, but her teacher would call on her at times, and Sarah would not always be able to answer the question. In fact, the teacher found that Sarah was not able to recall the question at all. When it was rephrased or repeated, she would often be able to answer correctly. Although Sarah was not a stellar student, she plugged along in second grade until April.

Sarah began giving her mother and father a hard time about coming to school. She was clearly not enjoying school. In class she seemed more and more tuned out. She had to have things reexplained often and, to keep up, looked more often at what the other students were doing. By this point in the year, her classmates were able to read and spell on a much more advanced level than Sarah.

Sarah's second-grade teacher referred her to the Child Study Team again. This time a complete educational evaluation was performed to find out the source of Sarah's difficulties. The psychologist found Sarah's IQ to be overall solidly in the average range for her age, but he did find that she needed to have the directions repeated, sometimes several times, before she would answer the questions. She also couldn't repeat a series of numbers (8–3–5–9) when asked, which could be symptomatic of an auditory memory problem. Sarah also showed some problems with drawing tasks and tasks that asked her to match shapes. Yet on other types of tasks, Sarah's scores were well above her age level. This kind of contrast (high scores in some areas, very low scores in others) in addition to Sarah's performance in the classroom and normal IQ indicated the presence of a learning disability.

The learning disabilities teacher found Sarah had a great deal of knowledge about many things. However, she clearly demonstrated difficulties with oral directions and sounding out words using her knowledge of phonics. When she saw a word she didn't know, she just guessed any word that began with the first letter.

The speech-language evaluation was also interesting. Sarah had an enormous vocabulary, naming even the more obscure pictures with ease. Her speech was clear and appropriate. Her stories were full of details but somewhat weak in organization. However, her biggest problem was auditory memory. When asked to repeat this sentence: "John gave his brother a large brown basket," she responded: "John's basket is brown." When asked to repeat this: "Each girl wore a pretty blue hat and white gloves," she said: "The girls had hats and . . . I forget." On all the sentences longer than this, she simply answered, "I forget." When asked to follow oral directions, she performed poorly. Similar results were exhibited on any task that asked her to listen to long pieces of information and answer questions about it.

Based on Sarah's test scores, her classroom performance, and behavior at home, she was diagnosed as having a learning disability, with auditory memory as a primary weakness. Sarah was able to receive help right in her classroom from the special education teacher and speech-language pathologist. Since there were several "problem listeners" in the classroom, lessons for improving listening were introduced each week to the whole class. The teacher modified the way she gave directions and presented new information. By adding these services and making some changes in the classroom, we were able to help Sarah enjoy school again. She is now a happy, although still sometimes challenged, fourth-grader.

Like all people with learning disabilities, Sarah will never be cured. However, she can learn successfully by using methods that are designed for her special needs.

The "I Don't Understand What I'm Supposed to Do" Child: A Language Processing Problem

I'm concerned about Manny. He's always been shy, but as he's getting older I'm beginning to think it's more than that. He's fine as long as he's playing with his friends or doing something physical, but he avoids conversations at all costs. He seems confused at times. I don't think he's a slow child, but he doesn't always seem to know what's going on. He's been defensive lately, which I'm not at all happy about. In school, he struggles to follow class discussions, and he often has no idea how to do his homework when he gets home. Thank goodness our neighbor is in the same class, because I'd never know what he's supposed to do. He reads well, but he doesn't seem to always understand what he read.

—Mother of Manny, age 8½

Children like Manny are more common than you think. Because he hasn't had serious behavior problems *yet* or struggled with reading or writing, Manny's problem has not stood out to his teachers or parents. Yet something is clearly not quite right, and his mother knows it. Is he "slow"? Is he simply a child who doesn't like conversations? Or is something else going on here?

In this section I discuss how to recognize and understand children with language processing problems and describe what can be done for them. Manny is exhibiting a classic *language processing disorder.* It causes him to have difficulty comprehending what people say. The words float around in his mind and need time to be "processed" by his brain before he can really understand them. When someone talks too fast or says too much at once, the thoughts get even more scrambled, and he can't make sense of any of it. This problem has several names, which tend to be used more or less interchangeably: *receptive language delay, auditory processing deficit,* or *auditory comprehension deficit.* However, I feel the term language processing problem best describes Manny's problem, because the words people use, the "language," is what is causing his confusion.

As with several of the other problems we've discussed, a language processing problem often goes hand in hand with other kinds of speech, language, and listening problems, or learning disabilities. If Manny had exhibited one of these other problems, he might have been diagnosed earlier, because the speech-language pathologist would have tested his language processing skills as part of an initial comprehensive evaluation. But since Manny belongs to the group of children whose primary problem is language processing, he avoided detection for some time. The effects of the problem are now slowly creeping into his life.

Children with language processing problems are easy to miss at younger ages because conversation is less complex and there are fewer listening demands. As children grow older, they are asked to process and use more and more language. Children's play begins to take the form of jokes and ribbing. They watch TV shows that require understanding of what the characters say and why they are saying it. Characters talk about how they feel; they argue, try to persuade, and come up with all kinds of crazy ideas and stories. In school, more and more lessons are centered on listening to the teacher explain math principles, science concepts, and so on, and to other students talk about any variety of things.

A child with a language processing disorder will miss a lot of information in all these situations. The following are some common problem areas for children with language processing disorders:

- *Humor.* It is very abstract and requires a higher level of processing. Children with language processing problems may not "get the joke."
- *Idioms.* These are expressions we use that, taken literally, mean something entirely different from the intended message. What does someone mean when they say they are "under the weather"? Does it mean it's going to rain? "Put yourself in my shoes" and "Get outta here!" are other examples.
- *Long, complicated directions.* These tend to get "tangled" in the child's mind. It isn't so much that he doesn't understand what it means to "write something on the top line," or "circle every word with a long vowel," or remember what to do, as with auditory memory problems. It's just that the child needs time to process one piece of information before the next one is given, or else he gets totally confused. This is also true when Manny's mother tells him to look in the "left side of the top drawer of Jessica's dresser for the pair of scissors." Too many positions (first, second, top, left, right, etc.) in one sentence are too much to process at once for him.
- *Stories with lots of characters and events.* Listening to these may get confusing. The problem also surfaces when you try to explain the family's vacation agenda or plans for the afternoon if it requires several stops, times, and people's names.

In many ways, reading is a listening task. As we read something, we actually say the words inside our minds. In effect, we listen to our own voices. If hearing lots of words at once makes the words become "jumbled up" in someone's mind, the same may happen when reading. We've all experienced this feeling when we've read something very technical and have had to reread the same passage several times before it really sinks in. The same is true when we're tired. You can read the same page over and over and really not "process" the information. You see it and hear it, but you do not comprehend it.

Language processing problems are diagnosed by observing a child in different listening situations as well as administering several standardized, formal tests. Does the child seem confused? Does the child frequently ask to have the teacher reexplain the directions or instructions for an assignment? Can the child listen to a story and understand what is happening?

In these cases, the speech-language pathologist has to act as a detective. Does the child have difficulty processing or comprehending the information because he doesn't know what certain words mean? For example, the child will easily become confused if a character fed a *kid* on the farm, if the word *kid* is not understood. Therefore, testing a child's vocabulary is an important part of understanding the root of his confusion.

Another skill the evaluator will want to check is the child's auditory memory, discussed earlier in this chapter. If the child can't remember what is being said, comprehending it will be difficult, if not impossible. Many times a child has a language processing *and* an auditory memory problem. The primary difference between the two problems is that the child with an auditory memory problem can comprehend and process what was said but quickly forgets it, perhaps even before responding. The incoming message jumps out of the child's mind. The child with a language processing problem doesn't comprehend what is said. The message is not received at all or not in the way it was intended. The child with a language processing problem misinterprets, rather than forgets, what was said.

Obviously, a hearing problem will also have to be ruled out. If certain other symptoms are present, the speech-language pathologist or other specialist may want to have an audiologist test for central auditory processing problems, discussed at the beginning of this chapter.

If a child has difficulty keeping her attention on one thing, an Attention Deficit Disorder (ADD) may cause her to function as though she has a language processing problem. In this type of case, treatment for ADD will improve the child's ability to focus on a message long enough to comprehend it.

In cases of children with mental retardation, language processing ability will always be affected, as are all language and listening skills. Weak language processing skills are part of a bigger, more global problem for a mentally retarded child, and it would not be appropriate to diagnose this child as having a language processing disorder per se.

Characteristics of Children with a Language Processing Problem

As with all speech, language, and listening problems, a child may manifest only one, or many, outward behaviors of a language processing problem. Children with a language processing disorder might do the following:

- Misunderstand or confuse what is being said
- Need directions explained several times and sometimes need demonstrations

- Need an unusual amount of time to think before answering a question
- Watch what everyone else is doing to figure out what to do
- Make comments that don't fit the discussion
- Take a long time to understand what is read or need to read a passage several times before understanding it
- Have difficulty answering questions that they know on a test, because the wording of the test question was hard to understand
- Have difficulty following the plot to a TV show or a movie; ask questions that reflect a lack of understanding of the critical points of the story
- Avoid participating in group or family conversations or discussions
- Have difficulty enjoying or appreciating humorous stories, anecdotes, or riddles, although they may often be the class clown
- Have other speech, language, listening, or learning disabilities
- Have a history of frequent middle ear infections
- Have unexplained behavior problems or dislike school
- Express the feeling that they are stupid
- Tune out or not pay attention during listening tasks

How Does a Language Processing Problem Affect a Child?

As we saw with Manny, a child with a language processing problem may eventually feel a bit left out and begin to react to that by avoiding or tuning out conversations. Children like Manny can feel very isolated when everyone in the group is laughing and they don't quite know why. "Maybe they're laughing at me?" You can see how easy it would be for Manny to become defensive or hostile when he doesn't quite understand what people are saying.

When everyone else is participating in an intense dinner table discussion, Manny might sit passively or begin playing with his food or his fork. With friends, he might unconsciously avoid conversational situations by initiating physical activities such as bike riding, playing tag, or roller skating. As he grows into a teenager, team sports or creative pursuits such as drawing, dancing, or music may become his focus.

Children who have self-esteem problems are already at risk for misinterpreting what people say to them or about them. Compound that with a language processing disorder and you may see a child who is very evasive or defensive during conversations, particularly when a confrontation or heated discussion is taking place. Feeling confused when your friends understand something tends to lower a child's self-esteem, which is why many children with this problem feel that they're stupid.

Sometimes children with a language processing problem make comments that are related to, but perhaps a little bit off, the topic you are talking about. That's because they are not quite sure what the point of the discussion is at times.

As discussed earlier, understanding humor is sometimes difficult for students with a language processing problem. That is not to say they are not funny. They can make *you* laugh in any number of ways, with slapstick (doing gross things or making faces) or making simple jokes. It's when someone else uses *language* to make a verbal joke, rather than, say, sticking straws up their nose, that they get thrown. You may see them laughing when everyone else does, but they really don't know what is so funny.

Because reading involves processing language, a child with this problem may have to read very slowly or need to read something several times before it makes sense. This can be a time-consuming chore, and children tend to get very anxious when they see everyone else on page 12, and they're still on page 8. So they may speed up, but they really do not understand what they're reading.

Taking tests can be frustrating for a child with a language processing problem. If the questions are read by the teacher orally, the child will be at a disadvantage because she may not have enough time to process the question before needing to write the answer. If the questions are written, they should be phrased clearly and simply, or the child may easily misinterpret what is being asked.

Children with mild language processing problems will need to work extra hard in school to keep up with the class, but it can be done. Choosing a career that takes advantage of a child's other strengths will be important.

Therapy for a Child with a Language Processing Disorder

Intervention for a child with a language processing problem depends on a number of factors. Are there other related problems, such as weak auditory memory or learning disabilities? How severe is the problem? How old is the child? In some cases, therapy may be appropriate to work on certain listening skills and improve a child's ability to process certain language forms, such as idioms or humor. Typically, children with mild problems are taught ways to compensate for the problem. These children are usually phased out of a formal program in a year or two. Like many forms of listening disorders, there is no cure for a language processing disorder, but children can certainly improve and develop their ability to process language through therapy and good teaching.

In a public school, the emphasis may need to be on adjusting the teacher's expectations and teaching style within the classroom rather than "fixing" the child. Since a language processing problem impacts the child's ability to take in information, the school may need to provide extra help or support in the classroom. Science, social studies, reading (comprehension), and other subjects may need to be retaught in small pieces on a simpler level. However, most schools do try to achieve this within the regular classroom with help from special education teachers, paraprofessionals, and/or the speech-language pathologist.

What Can Parents Do to Help a Child with a Language Processing Problem?

As with all speech, language, and listening problems, patience is an important virtue for any parent who has a child with a language processing disorder. You can help your child by keeping these thoughts in mind:

- Speak slowly. Children with processing problems can comprehend better when speakers slow down from their typical pace.
- Make sure your child is looking at you and "ready" to listen before you talk.
- Use body language and gestures to help make your point.
- Repeat and paraphrase important messages and ask questions to make sure your child has processed them. ("Be home by six o'clock. Make sure you're here by six o'clock. . . . When do you have to be home?")
- Pause between thoughts to allow time for your child to process the idea. ("After dinner, I'd like you to babysit Emma. . . . You can watch TV together or play a game. . . . Just make sure you're both in bed by 10:30.")
- Keep your sentences short. In other words, if you are upset with your child, say "I'm very upset right now. . . . What you did makes me unhappy," rather than "You know, every time I tell you to do something it seems you just do whatever you want. I'm very annoyed because what you did was totally uncalled for. . . ." etc.
- Encourage your child to ask questions when she doesn't understand. Children with a language processing problem already feel "dumb" at times, so they often hesitate to ask questions. Let your son or daughter know that asking questions shows a person is

listening and cares enough to really understand what someone is saying.

* Explain idioms, or other figurative language, if you use them or hear them being used with your child. Don't assume she knows what you mean when you say, "Keep a lid on it."

Case Study: Andre

Andre appeared to be a typical fourth-grade student in most respects. He was a B-C student in most subjects and had not presented a major concern to his past teachers, although several had expressed to me a feeling that something "just wasn't clicking" with him. When I asked them to file a formal referral, they usually backed down, saying he wasn't failing and that they had to deal with students with far more serious problems first.

However, by April, Andre's classroom teacher and his father were very concerned with his poor attitude. Andre was combative when asked to do assignments at home and goofed off in class instead of paying attention. He was having more and more trouble passing tests, but this was attributed to his poor attitude and lack of studying. A formal referral was filed in the hopes of engaging the assistance of the psychologist.

Andre received counseling for the rest of the year, and although he continued to struggle, he got through the rest of the year. In fifth grade, as he grew comfortable in counseling, Andre expressed feelings of "I'm dumb" more and more. The psychologist asked Andre's father for permission to do further testing. I requested permission for some testing to make sure Andre didn't have any other underlying language or listening problems, and the special education teacher also did some testing for learning disabilities.

The testing revealed Andre had a high-average IQ with strengths in many areas. However, his performance on listening tests revealed a significant problem with language processing. He understood what words meant when they were presented in isolation, but in the context of a paragraph or complex directions, he became very confused and frustrated. The learning disabilities testing showed problems with reading comprehension.

By making changes in how the teacher structured questions asked of Andre and in how information was presented to him, his stress level was reduced. Intervention by the special education teacher and speech-language pathologist helped him develop compensation strategies and function more effectively in the classroom. The psychologist continued to see Andre twice a month but was able to phase him out in a few months after Andre began his Individualized Educational Program (IEP) due to the improvement in Andre's behavior. As he began to feel more successful,

Andre's attitude began to change. He developed a new understanding of why he felt so stupid at times and began to take more pride in his superior math and art abilities. He stopped putting himself down and took chances in answering and asking questions. Since his homework was tailored to his individual needs, he was less resistant to doing it.

Andre, like the other children we've discussed, will never be cured of his language processing disorder. However, the effects of it were significantly minimized by the proper intervention and by his gaining a new understanding of himself. Andre is now the owner of a very successful plumbing business.

8

Causes and Conditions

Each child presents a unique set of abilities and challenges, many of which don't fit the textbook, or classic, profile. Although I have described many of the most common speech, language, and listening problems in previous chapters, there are many more that may be affecting your child. In this chapter, you will read about some of these causes of speech, language, and listening problems as well as special conditions that bring their own set of unique issues.

This chapter discusses serious topics such as abuse and neglect, lead poisoning, and oxygen loss to the brain. It also covers other problems that can often contribute to speech, language, and listening problems, such as frequent ear infections, mouth breathing, and thumb-sucking.

In addition, the chapter contains information on special conditions like Down syndrome, cleft palate, Attention Deficit Disorder, autism, and cerebral palsy. Many children with these handicaps have physical, mental, or medical conditions that require a great deal of attention or running back and forth to the doctor. Therefore, it's natural for parents to push aside things such as how well their child speaks or listens, especially when they are celebrating getting through the child's latest surgery. However, it is important to remember that helping children improve language and listening development will also have a profound effect on their future.

Common Causes of Speech, Language, and Listening Problems

Usually the first question a parent asks me after an evaluation is, "Does my child have a speech problem?" followed by, "Did I do something wrong?" I think, deep down, that is the fear of most parents whose child —the child they love with all their heart, the child they would die to protect—is not developing normally. Could they have unwittingly done this? The answer is usually no.

We in the speech-language pathology field focus our attention on determining a child's present speech and language skill level through an in-depth evaluation. This gives us valuable information that tells us how we can capitalize on the child's areas of strength as well as facilitate growth in the weaker areas. It also helps us to know which techniques will probably be more successful than others. The purpose of the evaluation is not to find fault with parents, make them feel guilty, or analyze marital problems or lifestyles.

Your speech-language pathologist may suggest *changes* in how you interact with your child to facilitate growth with certain skills, but you should never take this as a criticism of your parenting style. The goal is to make the most of the time you have with your child. Some children need a more aggressive approach than others. It doesn't mean what you've been doing is wrong; it merely means that your child has special needs that may require more attention, or a different kind of attention, from you than a typical child who is learning to speak. Other times, there may be contributing physical factors (such as orthodontic problems, hearing problems, and allergies) that need to be addressed before clear speech can be achieved.

Though it's rare, there are a few occasions where a parent can cause, or unknowingly contribute to a child's speech, language, or listening problems. In this chapter, I discuss what we know about these causes of some speech, language, and listening problems. I hope this section provides some reassurance, as well as advice, about how to avoid a similar problem in a younger sibling. Regrettably, there is still much to be done in the way of research on this topic. We don't have all the answers.

(In alphabetical order)

Abuse and Neglect

Perhaps the most frustrating cases we see as clinicians are children who came into this world with great potential or who *could have,* but do not, progress as expected because of their mother's or caregiver's actions. Communication problems in children can sometimes be caused or worsened by the following:

- Drug or alcohol abuse by the mother during pregnancy
- Poor prenatal nutrition
- Abuse by neglect—these are situations where babies and toddlers are basically left alone or in front of a TV set for the better part of their day; they may also be malnourished and are often removed from the home and placed in foster care by state agencies.
- Physical abuse—unfortunately, there are documented cases of children who have suffered brain damage from physical abuse by a parent, stepparent, or other caregiver.

As you can probably guess, the parents of these children, for a variety of reasons, are generally not apt to seek help for them. However, you may have adopted a child or care for a foster child whose problem is a result of these kinds of abusive behaviors. Or you may know someone whose child is at risk because of a substance abuse problem during pregnancy. These children need help right away because, although the odds are against them, with aggressive, early treatment, tremendous improvement *can* take place.

In speaking about "abuse by neglect," I am not referring to the amount of TV a typical child watches but about the television being used as a baby-sitter. Television programs can't ask questions or hold conversations with a child. Some educational programs on public television stations offer excellent benefits to the children who watch them, but someone needs to show interest in a child in order for meaningful language development to occur.

Apraxia

Some children have difficulty controlling their mouth muscles. The muscles are strong but seem to have a mind of their own. When children with apraxia are asked to open their mouth or stick out their tongue, they tend to take an extra amount of time and grope around while trying to figure out how to perform the requested action.

Blow to the Head (Brain Injury)

Many, if not most, children fall and hit their heads at some point in their childhood. This accident usually produces no ill effects or permanent brain damage. However, a blow to the head with just the right amount of force can cause the brain to swell, resulting in pressure and possible long-term effects on learning, behavior, and coordination. Such blows to the head are another cause of **traumatic brain injury,** which is discussed in greater detail later in this chapter. A severe enough blow or trauma to the skull can also make blood vessels burst, which can cause more specific damage to the brain.

If a child's skull is not fractured and consciousness is never lost, a hospital will often discharge or release the child, with a warning to watch the child. Unfortunately, the damage to the brain may be too subtle to detect at the time of the impact. Changes in behavior or language skills may incorrectly be attributed to the emotional impact of the incident, when, in fact, the child is displaying symptoms of a traumatic brain injury. If you have concerns about your child's recovery from one of these accidents, a neurologist is the most appropriate medical specialist to call. A pediatric neurologist can often be found at a children's hospital. Events that can bring on this type of injury include the following:

- Car accidents
- Falls or tumbles down the stairs
- Bicycle accidents
- Falls, with the head striking a rock or other hard object

Congenital Conditions

Some conditions are present at birth and predispose a child to speech and language delays. Some of these are Down syndrome, cerebral palsy, cleft palate, congenital deafness, and Hunter's syndrome (these are discussed later in this chapter). Sometimes a child loses oxygen during the birth process when the umbilical cord is wrapped around the neck or if the child temporarily loses heart function. Children born as a result of traumatic births following an incident such as the mother falling down a flight of stairs or being involved in a car accident should be watched carefully for later problems.

Premature babies are not necessarily at risk as they were years ago. With early intensive medical intervention and technology, premature babies without permanent birth defects can recover completely, catching up with their peers in a few years. Recent studies do not indicate any higher prevalence for language or learning problems for these children than for full-term children. However, if there was oxygen loss at birth, inadequate medical care, or other extenuating health issues, the risk does increase.

Fluctuating Hearing Loss from Frequent Ear Infections

Children who have had frequent ear infections in the first three years of life are at risk for speech and language delays. Defining "frequent" is difficult, but I would consider three or more infections in the first three years often enough for the child to be closely monitored. Many children referred for speech and language delays have a history of ear infections. Additionally, difficulty with remembering information (auditory memory) and understanding spoken information (auditory processing) may persist long after the hearing ability returns to normal.

Inherited or Imitated Family Speech and Language Deficits

It is not uncommon for a speech-language pathologist to treat brothers and sisters for similar speech problems. Whether this is due to nature or nurture has never been proven conclusively. It seems remarkable, though, that a child who is exposed to many, many different correct speech models (through friends, television, and neighbors) throughout the day would copy the one sibling whose speech pattern is distorted or agrammatical. Yet we do see these patterns in families happen sometimes.

The family patterns I have encountered tend to be mild articulation problems (lisps, distortions of *r* or *l*) and language delays or learning disabilities. Sometimes a parent also displays the same problem during our initial meeting and may or may not be aware of the connection. I have treated parents and children together for articulation problems when the parent initiates interest in correcting his or her own problem. It is not impossible to remediate a child's articulation problem if the parent continues to speak incorrectly, but it is more challenging!

Lead Poisoning

There is increasing evidence that lead poisoning is still a very serious problem in the United States. Your child does not have to eat chips of lead-based paint to become lead poisoned. Research shows that children are being poisoned by inhaling the dust in the air from lead-based paint or drinking water contaminated from lead pipes. A simple blood test can determine whether your child is suffering the effects from lead poisoning. Ask your doctor to perform this test if you are concerned. Your local health department may provide free screenings for this problem.

Lead-based paint was sold before 1974, when the federal government passed a law banning it. This paint can be disturbed merely by opening and closing a window with an old coat of paint on it. When renovations are done on an old home, lead-based paint is often disturbed. Visiting an older home undergoing renovations for a long weekend can be enough to cause a problem, if only temporarily. However, even short exposures *can* have long-term repercussions for a child.

A child only needs to inhale a small amount of contaminated air in order to be poisoned. If the lead problem is not corrected, the poisoning can soon result in permanent learning and behavior disorders. Children under the age of 6 are considered to be at the greatest risk for lead poisoning. The adults in the same home may have no symptoms at all, because their bodies can fight off the lead poisoning more easily. A child with lead poisoning will typically become agitated and cranky and may in time develop attention deficit problems and learning disabilities (including language problems) if the lead source is not identified and removed. Early detection and removal of the source will prevent permanent problems.

Lead pipes can also contaminate your water source. Before buying a house, have the water in your home checked for lead, even if it is not mandated by your state real estate laws. If your child is found to have lead poisoning, you will need to locate the source. Don't forget to have your water examined for a high lead content.

The Centers for Disease Control in Atlanta at (404) 639-3311 can refer you to proper resources and current pamphlets on this subject.

Limited or Low Intellectual Ability

This is a difficult diagnosis to make at a young age, because intellectual testing is often unreliable, except on a gross scale, before the age of 7. This is one reason school systems tend to call all children who are behind their peers in two or more areas before this age developmentally delayed unless a physician makes a more specific diagnosis. These children have difficulty in most, or all, developmental areas. They typically have delayed milestones for nonspeech skills, such as walking, playing appropriately, manipulating puzzles, and self-care such as dressing and feeding themselves. Sometimes they do these things at the proper age, but the quality of their skills is poor. Retarded children do not ever catch up, no matter how much intervention they receive, but their prognosis is much improved with early and appropriate therapy. Depending on the degree of their deficits, they are sometimes later labeled slow learner, educable mentally retarded, minimally brain-damaged, trainable retarded, or profoundly retarded. Speech, language, and listening will be a lifelong challenge for these children. Today's public educational system, however, is staffed and trained to accommodate and develop *every* child's skills to the highest possible level. You can, and should, take advantage of every opportunity to help your child achieve the most he or she can.

Lip Muscle Weakness

When a child has weak lip muscles, certain sounds, such as *p, b, m, f,* and *v,* are difficult to pronounce because the lips must move to make these sounds. The same muscles are used for puckering when sucking liquids through a straw, blowing, and breathing through the nose with the lips together. When a child has difficulty pronouncing these sounds, lip exercises and other nonspeech (oral-motor) activities may be necessary to build up the muscles.

Mouth Breathing

A child with ongoing allergies often finds it difficult to breathe through the nose, forcing him into the habit of breathing through the mouth. Enlarged adenoids or tonsils can contribute to the problem. Breathing through the mouth causes the tongue muscles to become off balance, in a forward position. Children who consistently breathe through their mouth sometimes develop a "lispy" quality when pronouncing words with sounds such as *s* and *z,* because their tongue hangs forward between their teeth. Therapy to correct the lisp typically is more effective if the child's nasal passages are cleared and breathing through the nose is relearned. If the child's tongue muscles have had a long time to become unbalanced, a forward swallowing pattern may also need remediation before the lisp can be successfully corrected.

Oxygen Loss from Trauma

If your child's oxygen supply is restricted, even for a short time, permanent brain damage can occur. This is another type of *traumatic brain injury* (TBI). Traumatic brain injury is exhibited by a regression or lack of improvement in your child's speech and language skills. In infants, TBI is more difficult to detect by behavior alone. You may find your child's crying patterns to be different, eye gaze less focused, and general alertness changed. A neurologist is the medical specialist who can tell you whether your child has suffered brain damage as a result of this type of trauma. If your child has experienced one of the following events, the attending physician will undoubtedly also know to check for this. Some events that cause a loss of oxygen to the brain include the following:

- Near drowning
- Near suffocation
- Reaction to a medical procedure
- Choking
- Temporary loss of heart function or pulse

For more information about speech, language, and listening issues related to traumatic brain injury, please refer to this heading later in the chapter under "Autism, Cerebral Palsy, Hearing Impairment, and Other Special Conditions."

Restricted Tissue under the Tongue

Sometimes children have difficulty moving their tongue freely because it is anchored too tightly. This condition is called *anklyoglossia* (also known as tongue tie), or in less severe cases, a shortened frenum. These conditions are easily corrected with simple oral surgery. As a result, the child can speak more comfortably and clearly. Sometimes tongue exercises and speech therapy are necessary after the procedure to help the tongue learn how to move to pronounce certain sounds. Typically, an *r* sound is affected because it requires the tongue to retract backward in the mouth. The speech overall may have a "mumbly" quality to it, as though the tongue is labored or restricted. A child with anklyoglossia may also have some difficulty chewing and swallowing a variety of textures of food comfortably.

Seizures

Children with a history of seizures, whether from a high fever, an unknown origin, or a seizure disorder such as epilepsy, are at greater risk for developing language deficits. Sometimes a baby or toddler may even show a regression in language development for a period of time following the seizure. Often speech, language, and listening functioning may improve or resume its previous level with time. However, repeated seizures can sometimes result in permanent brain damage, which could have an impact on a child's speech, language, and listening skills.

Thumb-Sucking and Bottle-Feeding Past Age One

Many children suck their thumb or use bottles sporadically past the age of 1 with no apparent long-term effect on their speech. However, if a child does so on a daily, consistent basis, the habit can often cause the tongue and lip muscles to become off balance, resulting in a tongue thrust. These habits can also push the front teeth forward and cause future orthodontic problems. Tongue thrusting can result in a distortion of the s and z sounds. *Sh, ch,* and *j* can also be affected. When the child tries to pronounce these sounds, the tongue pushes between the upper and lower teeth as when making a *th* sound, instead of the correct sounds. Unless your child is on a special feeding program under the supervision of an occupational therapist or speech therapist, try to wean your child onto a regular cup by age 1.

Teeth Misalignment, Jaw Movements, and Missing Teeth

When a child has untreated orthodontic problems, it sometimes will make pronouncing words difficult. For example, a significant overbite, crossbite, or underbite may cause certain sounds to be difficult to pronounce clearly. If, in addition, the child has a high, narrow palate and/ or a tongue thrust, these factors can work together to make certain movements necessary for speech difficult. In most cases, a speech pathologist can help the child find another way to make the same sounds until the problem can be corrected. If this approach is unsuccessful, it may make sense to wait until the child's orthodontic problems have been addressed. During the orthodontic process, the child may have a large appliance for palate widening installed in the mouth, which would further hinder clear speech and make waiting an appropriate course of action.

Crooked teeth, as a general rule, do not interfere with speech production.

When a child has missing front teeth, some sounds, such as *f* and *s*, are slightly distorted until the new teeth grow in.

In some cases, a child may have an adequate bite but may still demonstrate difficulty with appropriate jaw movements during eating and speaking. If a child slides the jaw from left to right or favors eating on one side, there may be a problem with the jaw muscles. Because the tongue is rooted in the lower jaw, where it goes is directly determined by where the jaw goes. If a child's jaw is not coming together in the correct way, the tongue will not go to the appropriate position when speaking. In these cases, the speech pathologist will need to utilize oral-motor therapy to help the child use these muscles correctly when eating and speaking.

Tongue Muscle Weakness

The tongue is probably the single most important muscle used when speaking. If a child is not able to lift it or move it where it needs to go, speaking will be difficult. The child may also have difficulty chewing food and swallowing, which sometimes results in frequent choking and, consequently, the need for a restricted diet. For this reason, a child with weak tongue muscles should work on nonspeech (oral-motor) activities to strengthen the tongue muscles for speech.

Unknown Causes

For many children, speech, language, and listening delays emerge for little apparent reason over time, becoming more noticeable at the age of 18 months to 4 years of age, depending on the severity of the delay. Less severe communication deficits such as articulation problems, stuttering, voice disorders, and processing difficulties may be less noticeable or absent at this young age. It is not uncommon for them to go undetected until sometime in the elementary school years.

As speech-language pathologists, we do our best to pin down the cause of the problem. However, we accept that *in many, if not most, cases, we never know why a child's speech, language, and listening develop differently or more slowly than the average child's.*

Autism, Cerebral Palsy, Hearing Impairment, and Other Special Conditions

For some children, speech, language, and listening are particularly challenging tasks. When a child is born with, or acquires, physical or mental handicaps, it is the beginning of a new and sometimes daunting journey for the parent. What will happen to my child? Will she ever be able to communicate the way other children do? What should I do to help my child make the most of these developmental years? These are natural questions to ponder. Unfortunately, most of these questions are not easily answered at birth or in general terms. The old axiom "Each child is unique" really does hold true.

For example, ten people with Down syndrome can speak and function on ten different ability levels by the time they reach their 20th birthday. Some people with Down syndrome grow up, work, and even marry. Others need more help with day-to-day activities, speak with great difficulty, and are less independent. Although there are common bonds that tie certain groups of children, what one child needs may be different from what another child needs. Education and speech-language therapy is not a one-size-fits-all proposition.

Only time will tell what the future holds for a child with one of these conditions. For now, parents can help their child make the most of all the special help and experiences life has to offer. Attitudes have changed in the past few years toward children with handicaps and special challenges. They have access to all kinds of therapies and technology that can make a big difference in their quality of life. Thus, they can enjoy their childhood and do most of the things that any "normal" child can do.

In this section I briefly outline the nature of some special conditions and the associated speech, language, and listening issues of each, along with a short discussion of what kind of intervention you might expect. Your child's doctor makes the diagnosis as to whether or not your child has one of these conditions. Although there are hundreds of neurological, muscular, and intellectual conditions and syndromes, I have selected the most common in the interest of space.

If your child has a special condition not described here, the American Speech-Language-Hearing Association can put you in touch with a specialist in your area who might be able to answer your questions. Phone numbers and addresses are included in Appendix A. Many other organizations, public and private, that are devoted to helping children with handicaps are listed also.

Attention Deficit Problems

Some children that come to see me are very bright yet have difficulty staying on-task. Their minds are quickly and furiously checking out the pictures on the walls, the games on my shelves, and the objects on my desk. They want to touch and experience them all, and all at once. Everything distracts them, even themselves, though never intentionally. In recent years, the term Attention Deficit Disorder (ADD) has been used to describe this condition. Sometimes children with ADD are also hyperactive (ADHD); sometimes they are not. When a child has an attention deficit problem, listening and attending to a conversation or classroom lecture is difficult. In a quiet room at home the problem may be less noticeable. But because a classroom is decorated with colorful posters, has the sounds of pencils being sharpened, and so on, these children have far more difficulty getting work done in school.

Most children with ADD function as though they have auditory memory and language processing problems. This is because the information they hear is not "getting in." Children with ADD tune out someone's voice and focus on another sound or something they can see, such as a bird or squirrel in a tree out a nearby window. They can't remember or process a message that is not received in the first place. With medication (usually Ritalin), physical maturation, and the use of coping strategies, children with ADD can improve their listening skills. However, listening and staying focused on someone speaking will probably always be a challenge for these children, even into adulthood.

Another issue for children with ADD is taking turns in a conversation or classroom discussion. They are typically the children who call out answers and forget to raise their hand. They may sometimes repeat an answer someone else said or answer a previous question. This is not due to rudeness or insubordination. Rather, a child with ADD is typically impulsive by nature and acts quickly, without being able to process what other people say or wait for their turn. If they wait too long, their brain will have moved on to another thought by the time the teacher calls on them. When they do raise their hand, they will often say "I forgot" when the teacher asks them for their response.

In conversations, children with ADD may also have some difficulty at times keeping focused on the topic being discussed. They often digress from the question you ask and go off on many other related tangents. They may ramble and tell events out of sequence. They may interrupt the other person speaking, particularly at inappropriate times. Although they may be poor communicators at times for the reasons discussed, they may not necessarily have a language disorder, in the traditional sense of the term, in addition to their attention span problem. Sometimes they do. The two are so closely intertwined, it often may be difficult to tell. But because a child with ADD functions as a child with a listening and/or language problem does, the same suggestions for parents presented in chapters 6 and 7 hold true.

Autism

Autism is diagnosed by observing certain behaviors, usually in the child's first three years of life. The child may seem disconnected from people. An autistic child may not speak at all or may repeat what is heard in an echoing manner (**echolalia**) like a tape recorder, yet not say "Mama" or "Dada" with meaning yet. A child with autism generally likes routine and predictability—sameness. Busy and loud environments may be overstimulating and discomforting to an autistic child. Autism is now generally accepted to be a biologically based disorder of an unknown origin, which means no one caused it to happen.

There is a wide range of abilities and expectations for a child with autism. Some children are severely affected. Other children with **Asberger syndrome,** a mild form of autism, may simply strike you as "odd," having poor eye contact and little regard or understanding of normal social interactions. In fact, poor social use and understanding of language (pragmatics) are the hallmarks of an autistic child.

Children with autism might do the following:

- Seem "deaf" at times, tuning out both sounds and people talking
- Repeat things out of context, such as a TV commercial dialogue or words to a song
- Use jargon instead of real words
- Repeat a question asked, or the last part of it, instead of answering it
- React to sounds such as blenders, lawnmowers, and so on, as though they are painful, by putting their hands over their ears, crying, or screaming
- Not follow the normal pattern of language development; may use complex sentences before being able to name common objects in a baby book
- Speak with an unusual and unnatural intonation pattern; may sound robotic or "sing-song"
- Have difficulty performing or attending to tasks such as pointing to pictures named or naming pictures in a book on command
- Have difficulty comprehending what people say
- Have difficulty understanding or using facial expressions normally
- Have difficulty initiating or maintaining any kind of normal conversation or interaction

Many different approaches are used to help children with autism learn to communicate. Since the late 1980s some therapists report success with a technique called **facilitated communication.** This involves supporting the child's hand or arm on a keyboard (or picture of a keyboard) while the child points to the letters, which form words and sentences. (Autistic children do often possess, from a very early age, good reading and spelling skills, even though never formally taught, as well as the ability to tell time and do math.) The validity and reliability of the facilitated communication technique, however, is being hotly debated. Research is starting to show that in many cases there is unintentional, but clear, influence on the part of the facilitator.

Another new area of interest is **Auditory Integration Therapy**

(AIT), which is conducted by a few specially trained people. The training takes place over several weeks and is designed to reduce a child's intolerance to noise and sound, which is frequently associated with crankiness or even screaming. It is also reported (although not proven with substantial research) to help improve a child's tolerance of his or her own voice, resulting in increased language use. I worked directly with a child who underwent the Berard method of this training and can report substantial language changes and growth within weeks of completing the training. Information on this training can be obtained through ASHA, listed in Appendix A.

The most important aspect of any speech or language program for an autistic child is creating and facilitating opportunities for social interaction. More and more, autistic children are being successfully integrated into regular classrooms, which provide a more appropriate setting for social learning for many children. Autistic children need a clear expectation of what to say and do in every social situation. Practicing these social rituals and even creating cue cards sometimes helps. Other activities should help develop listening and reading comprehension skills and basic naming and explaining.

Parents should work closely with the teachers and help the child enjoy as many normal activities as possible. Keep to a routine. If you are not sure your child understands you, write down what you say, as you say it. Give him time to read it again and process it. Even though your child often seems distracted or turned away, information often "goes in." Autistic children have serious listening problems. When in doubt, write!

Cerebral Palsy

Cerebral palsy (also known as CP) is a descriptive term for a group of disorders that affect the way a child moves. It is caused by brain damage that occurs during fetal development or at birth. Sometimes other learning problems are present as a result. Cerebral palsy is not progressive; that is, it doesn't get worse as the child grows up. It can affect one or more limbs, as well as the muscles on the face, and, with most disorders, there is a wide range of disability. With very mild cases, the child may have a limp; in more severe cases, the child needs to use a wheelchair.

There are several types of cerebral palsy, and an individual often has more than one type. With *spastic cerebral palsy,* the child's muscles make jerky movements and contract too hard. A child with *athetoid cerebral palsy* has involuntary contractions, which result in shaking or swinging of various parts of the body. Eighty percent of cerebral palsy cases are of these two types (Van Riper, 1978).

You can imagine how difficult it would be to speak if you couldn't move your mouth the way you wanted to. A child with cerebral palsy will have difficulty using the tongue and lips not only for speaking but also for chewing and swallowing. Involuntary drooling and grimacing often result as well. Although therapy will help develop and strengthen the oral-motor skills needed for talking, chewing, and swallowing, little can be done at this writing to undo the brain damage that causes the problem. There is a certain amount of acceptance that needs to come with a child who has cerebral palsy. The goal of therapy is not to cure the child but to make the most of the child's abilities.

One of the biggest problems children with cerebral palsy have is using their chest muscles and lungs to push out enough air, at the right time, for speaking. A lot of coordination is involved in this task. Many times the child will open the mouth but nothing will come out. Or she will run out of air before finishing the thought, ending in a whisper. Exercises to improve the strength and coordination of these muscles is important for a child with cerebral palsy.

The speech pattern of the typical child with cerebral palsy is described as **dysarthric**—a slurring, labored, imprecise manner of speaking characteristic of brain damage. Again, speech patterns can be improved with speech therapy to a certain extent, but the child will never have perfectly clear articulation. A good goal is for the child to be understandable to others.

A child with cerebral palsy tends to have a different voice quality as well. Because the muscles in the throat shape the voice, a child who overcontracts or has weakened muscles will most likely sound somewhat nasal or explosive. The pauses in the child's speech may sound like a stutterer's hesitation, but the lack of fluency is also due to the difficulty with controlling muscles.

Sometimes a child with cerebral palsy is affected severely. As a result, speech is simply not a feasible form of communication. A host of recent, creative technological advances have created many more opportunities for a nonverbal child to communicate. With eye blinks or a touch, the child can operate many of the devices. When a child uses another form of communication, it is called **augmentative and alternative communication (AAC).** Today there are young adults with cerebral palsy who, although they are unable to speak, attend college and write fantastic stories.

Cleft Palate

A **cleft palate,** a deformity that is present at birth, is a physical problem characterized by an opening on the roof of the mouth that leads into the nasal cavity. Children with a cleft palate sometimes also have a cleft of the lip. A cleft lip usually involves the top part of the lip, which seems split in half, up to the nose. A child with a cleft palate can be at risk for developing middle ear infections, resulting in a temporary hearing loss. Teeth are often significantly misaligned, requiring extensive orthodontics. Until corrected with surgery or fitted with an appliance, a child with a cleft palate will have significant difficulty swallowing food or drinking.

Treatment of a child with a cleft palate requires extensive specialized care from a good craniofacial (skull and face) team at a hospital. The child may require several surgeries to repair the opening, but the doctors must wait to complete the task until the child has finished most, or all, growth. A surgeon, dentist, speech pathologist, orthodontist, and prosthodontist all need to work together on this team. The prosthodontist fits the child with an appliance called an **obturator,** which fits over the hole in the palate so the child can speak more clearly and eat more easily. This needs to be readjusted and replaced as the child grows. Some children use an obturator temporarily; others need one permanently because the tissue in the mouth or throat is not sufficient, even with surgery, for clear speech or easy swallowing.

A child with a cleft palate will need intensive speech therapy from a very early age. The hospital will usually make arrangements for this. Later, in the United States, the public school will provide therapy. The child's speech is characterized by a nasal quality, as though talking through the nose instead of the mouth. Certain sounds, such as *p, b, t, d, k,* and *g,* are difficult to pronounce. Often the child will make a snorting sound with the nose while talking. Many preschool-age children with cleft palates are extremely difficult to understand. Some children, despite the best medical attention and therapy, still speak with noticeable difficulty. Fortunately, new advances are occurring in the field every day.

Down Syndrome

Down syndrome, previously called mongolism, is a specific form of retardation. It is genetic, not caused by something the mother did or didn't do during pregnancy. Having a child with Down syndrome is a higher risk when a woman gives birth over the age of 35 and a slightly higher risk when the father is 45 to 50 and older. As with most syndromes, there is a very wide range of ability within the Down syndrome population. Some children are merely "slow" and have a fairly typical childhood; others are severely retarded, unable to communicate easily or care for themselves. Most children with Down syndrome function in the mild to moderately retarded range.

A child with Down syndrome has certain physical traits that help the doctor make the diagnosis at birth. The head, ears, mouth, and nose of the child are somewhat smaller than those of a typical child. The eyelids are narrow and slanted. There are often white specks on the outside edges of the iris (colored) part of the eye. The top of the ear sometimes folds over slightly, and the inside of the ear, the canal, is narrow. Often children with Down syndrome have a tongue thrust, meaning their tongue protrudes when speaking and swallowing. Lips get very dry and chapped. About half of the children with Down syndrome have a crease across each hand, and about 40 percent have some kind of heart defect. These children are also prone to frequent middle ear infections and colds.

Because Down syndrome is nearly always identified at birth or shortly thereafter, important early intervention is possible. Parents in the United States and Canada can take advantage of programs that help stimulate the child's development in all areas from infancy. The child will be delayed in walking and crawling, as well as talking. During infancy, therapy may be in the home or at a hospital. Preschool programs that combine these activities into a play-oriented setting are particularly effective.

It is becoming increasingly commonplace in the United States and Canada (and in my opinion, desirable, if it is possible, particularly in the preschool and elementary years) to educate children with Down syndrome in a regular classroom. This practice is called the **inclusion** model. However, the child will need much assistance and individualization to keep progressing with his or her own goals, which may be somewhat different from those of the other children. By being placed with typical children, the child will have good speech role models and more opportunity to practice speaking and communicating than when in a classroom with children who don't communicate well.

Children with Down syndrome may not necessarily need the usual speech therapy from a speech-language pathologist. Often the parent and teachers can work together to provide the type of stimulation that will benefit the child most. The speech pathologist may be asked to act as a consultant or monitor. This is particularly true if the child's speech and language skills are functional and balanced with the other aspects of their development or once the child has reached a plateau in adolescence.

Some children with Down syndrome have specific speech or language problems that are more complex than a simple delay in development. If the child is not able to be understood most of the time after the age of 5 or so, speech therapy may be appropriate and necessary. The parents and teachers will need to work closely with the speech pathologist, because integrating the skills into everyday speaking settings is a challenge for the child with Down syndrome. For this reason, it is helpful if the speech pathologist can work in the child's home or classroom for at least part of the time.

Many children will initially need the quiet and distraction-free environment of the speech room to attend to the therapy and learn the skills. Another reason why some speech therapy may need to take place outside the regular classroom is because the play and hands-on nature of the speech-language activities makes them sometimes difficult to conduct in the regular classroom if academic lessons are taking place. Speech is often, and should be, a noisy activity if done correctly. Usually most formal speech-language therapy is phased out after adolescence or once the child has stopped making measurable progress.

The important thing to remember is there is no *one* right way to teach a child with Down syndrome. Each child is unique.

Hearing Impairment and Deafness

Deafness implies a child cannot hear sound at all, or very little, even with a hearing aid. *Hearing-impaired* means a child can hear some sound. Some children with mild hearing impairments function well with a hearing aid; others exhibit serious speech, language, and listening problems. Children with moderate to severe hearing impairments struggle with speaking clearly and comprehending speech. Children who have fluctuating hearing loss from chronic middle ear infections (otitis media) during infancy and preschool years are at risk for impairments of speech and language, which can create problems for learning and functioning in school (Friel-Patti & Finitzo, 1990). *Middle ear infections are the most common cause of acquired hearing loss in children from birth to 3 years of age* (Garrard & Clark, 1985). Impairment can occur in one or both ears.

There are many other causes for hearing-related problems, ranging from a virus during the mother's pregnancy to a case of meningitis contracted by the child. Many times there is no known cause. It just happens.

A child identified at birth as deaf is fortunate in many ways. Diagnosing deafness and hearing impairment as soon as possible is half the battle. Years ago, children sometimes went undiagnosed for several years. This is less common now, but it still happens. Getting the child a hearing aid as soon as possible will help him listen and imitate speech.

Even with the hearing aid, most children will need a rather aggressive speech and auditory therapy program for many years if understandable speech or functional listening is the goal.

For some deaf children, speaking and listening is not an obtainable, or even desirable, goal. Many members of the deaf community feel strongly that deaf children should be taught to use sign language as soon as possible and should be educated with other deaf children. Others, who feel that using sign language impedes the deaf child's progress in learning to speak, work aggressively to help the child use whatever hearing he has in learning to speak and listen. Some professionals use a combined approach, called *total communication.* The long-term goal of the total communication philosophy of teaching is for the child to be able to function in the deaf community as well as the hearing community. Again, there is no one right way to teach a deaf child. The approach largely depends on the parents' philosophy, the hearing of the child, and the philosophy of the professionals who work with the child.

A new surgically implanted device has been designed that allows some deaf children to hear some sound. It is called a *cochlear implant* and is placed under the child's skin above the ear. The child wears a small box on a belt or harness, which is wired to a magnet that is attached to the skin over the implant. The child can remove the box and wires when bathing or running around.

This procedure has only been available since the early 1990s and is not available in all areas, nor is it appropriate for all deaf children. Results with the cochlear implant vary from child to child, depending on the type of implant used, the follow-up care and therapy, and the ability of the child. Candidates for the cochlear implant are carefully screened and evaluated before the decision to perform the surgery is made. Some parents do not wish for their child to go through this surgery (which, like any surgical procedure, has some inherent risk) and are content to let their child live as a deaf child. I have been working with a child who has a cochlear implant and can tell you he has progressed from saying a few words such as *Mommy* to speaking in short, fairly understandable sentences in less than two years. When his cochlear implant is turned off, he cannot hear a single sound. I feel it has opened up a whole new world for him and has given him the tools to do almost anything he wants in this life.

A deaf child may be able to function quite well in a normal classroom with the help of an interpreter, who can sign what the teacher is saying. For this child, "listening" is done by watching someone's hands. "Speaking" is communicating with one's hands. The greatest challenge for a child who signs will be to comprehend reading material and to write sentences grammatically. Sign language does not follow English grammar rules precisely, so reading and writing are difficult concepts for the deaf child to grasp.

Children with even mild hearing impairments have problems with pronunciation. Certain sounds, such as *s*, *sh*, and *t*, may be difficult to hear, so the child may not pronounce them at all unless taught how. A sentence might sound like this: "My i-uh i nie" (My sister is nice). Sounds heard at the ends of words, which are harder to hear, are often left off. A hearing-impaired child's voice has a peculiar "sound" to it, as though it is coming from the back of the throat, and is deeper pitched. In contrast, deaf children tend to have high-pitched voices. Sentence structures are typically characterized by the omission of small words (*the, a, is, to*). A sentence might be put together this way: "Boy rode horse." Aggressive speech therapy and proper amplification, as early as possible, will help improve these skills.

When listening, a child with even a mild hearing problem will have difficulty remembering directions or other information heard. When there is background noise, listening is difficult and tiring, so the child is often distracted. Interestingly, when the child wears a hearing aid, the problem is intensified because the hearing aid amplifies *every* noise. Learning phonics may be difficult because the child's discrimination for sounds is affected. Following an oral conversation may be confusing. Speech therapy for children with heaing problems also addresses improving their ability to comprehend and remember what is said.

As mentioned previously, a device called an FM system is particularly useful in helping a child with any permanent or temporary hearing problem function in the classroom (see chapter 7). In the United States, a child with a hearing impairment should have an FM system listed on the child's IEP, which means the school should pay for it. It is a basic piece of equipment that will help the child function successfully in the regular classroom and costs between $1,000 to $1,500, depending on the model and needs of the child.

The majority of deaf and hearing-impaired children do have lifelong delays in speech, language, and (obviously) listening abilities. However, there is much we can do today to minimize the impact of a hearing problem and help the child develop to the fullest possible potential.

Traumatic Brain Injury

A *traumatic brain injury* (TBI) occurs when there is damage to the brain after birth from a specific event, such as a blow to the head, near drowning, choking, or deprivation of oxygen to the brain. Children with traumatic brain injuries display certain language and listening problems (aphasia) during their recovery and even permanently in many cases. The recovery period can last at least a year or even a little longer. It is often difficult for the parent of a child with a brain injury to see the child struggle to perform simple tasks that were done before with ease. At the same time, the parent can rejoice that the child's life was saved. Years ago, many children with TBI did not survive. Progress in a recovering child is often amazingly rapid, although a complete recovery is often not possible.

Children with TBI often display particular speech, language, and listening characteristics. They might do the following:

- Have difficulty concentrating or paying attention
- Have difficulty with listening skills: memory, comprehension, and processing
- Have difficulty talking about one subject; tend to ramble from thought to thought with little organization or sequence
- Have difficulty interacting in an appropriate way socially; may say things that are embarrassing or completely fictional
- Have difficulty putting complex or grammatical sentences together, especially at first
- Have difficulty thinking of the names of common objects (**anomia**)
- Have difficulty moving the lips, tongue, and jaw as desired
- Have difficulty pronouncing words with precision, mixing up syllables
- Use a monotonous pitch or odd intonation pattern when speaking

A child with a traumatic brain injury has other medical and therapeutic issues to deal with, aside from speech and language. Learning how to walk, tie a shoe, and adjust to such a drastic change in functioning are just a few tasks they must cope with. Children with traumatic brain injuries and their families work with a team of specialists that helps them along the long rehabilitative road. A neurologist, psychologist, occupational therapist, and physical therapist are just a few of the members of the team.

How a child's brain thinks is called *cognitive functioning*. Attention span, memory, problem solving, and social judgment are cognitive skills. These are also important areas of relearning important to a child with a traumatic brain injury.

After a child with TBI has been released from the hospital or rehabilitation hospital, reentering school is possible with a great deal of support and understanding. Often the child does not understand that she is different. Denial is part of the brain injury. For this reason, the child may resist going to therapies or receiving special help. The parent and psychologist can help the child deal with these feelings of resentment.

The nature and amount of the therapy to address speech, language, and listening depend on the degree of the injury, the time elapsed since the injury, and the age of the child.

Appendix A

Resources

The following organizations and agencies may be able to give you additional information about your child's speech, language, or listening problem or direct you to a local agency that can help you.

For information about speech-language-hearing services in the United States:

American Speech-Language-Hearing Association (ASHA)
10801 Rockville Pike
Rockville, MD 20852
(301) 897-0457

National Association for Hearing and Speech Action (NAHSA)
10801 Rockville Pike
Rockville, MD 20850
(301) 897-8682 (Voice/TDD)
(800) 638-8255 (Voice/TDD)

National Institute of Neurological and Communication Disorders and Stroke
National Institutes of Health

Building 31A, Room 8A-06
Bethesda, MD 20892

For information about speech-language-hearing services in Canada:

The Canadian Association of Speech-Language Pathologists and Audiologists (CASLPA)
1215-25 Main St. West
Hamilton, Ontario L8P 1H1
(905) 523-5790
FAX (905) 523-5792

For information about any kind of disability and parents' rights in the United States:

Accent on Information (AOI)
P.O. Box 700

Bloomington, IL 61702
(309) 378-2961

The Council for Exceptional Children
(CEC)
1920 Association Drive
Reston, VA 22091
(703) 620-3660

Disability Rights Education & Defense
Fund, Inc.
1616 P Street, NW
Suite 100
Washington, DC 20036
(202) 328-5185

Education Resources Information
Center
Central ERIC
National Institute of Education
U.S. Department of Education
Washington, DC 20208
(202) 254-7934

National Information Center for
Children and Youth with
Disabilties
P.O. Box 1492
Washington, DC 20013
(703) 893-6061
(800) 999-5599

National Information Center for
Children and Youth with
Handicaps (NICHCY)
P.O. Box 1492
Washington, DC 20013
(800) 999-5599

National Institute on Deafness and
Other Communication Disorders
Clearinghouse (NIDCD)
Building 31, Room 3C-35
9000 Rockville Pike
Bethesda, Maryland 20892
(301) 496-7243
(800) 241-1044
FAX (800) 241-1055

Magazine for families and parents of children with disabilities:

Exceptional Parent Magazine
605 Commonwealth Ave.

Boston, MA 02215
(800) 247-8080

For information about Attention Deficit Disorder (ADD):

Children and Adults with Attention
Deficit Disorder (CHADD)
499 NW 70th Avenue
Suite 308
Plantation, FL 33317
(305) 587-3700

For information about autism:

Autism Society of America
7910 Woodmont Avenue
Suite 650
Bethesda, MD 20814
(301) 565-0433
(800) 3-Autism

National Society for Autistic Children
8601 Georgia Avenue
Suite 503
Silver Spring, MD 20910
(301) 565-0433

For information about cerebral palsy:

National Easter Seal Society
2023 West Ogden Avenue
Chicago, IL 60612
(312) 243-8400
(800) 221-6827

United Cerebral Palsy Association,
Inc.
1522 K Street, NW
Suite 1112
Washington, DC 20005
(800) 872-5827

For information about cleft palate and other facial deformities:

American Cleft-Palate-Craniofacial
Association/American Cleft Palate
Foundation

1218 Grand View Avenue
Pittsburgh, PA 15211
(412) 481-1376
(800) 24-CLEFT

For information about the deaf or hard of hearing:

Alexander Graham Bell Association
for the Deaf
3417 Volta Place, NW
Washington, DC 20007
(202) 337-5220

American Society for Deaf Children
814 Thayer Avenue
Silver Spring, MD 20910
(301) 585-5400 (Voice/TDD)
(800) 942-2732

National Information Center on
Deafness
Gallaudet University
800 Florida Avenue
Washington, DC 20002
(202) 651-5051

For information about learning disabilities:

Foundation for Children with
Learning Disabilities (FCLD)
99 Park Ave.
New York, NY 10016
(212) 687-7211

Learning Disabilities Association of
America (LDA)
4156 Library Road
Pittsburgh, PA 15234
(412) 341-8077
(412) 341-1515

Orton Dyslexia Society
The Chester Building
8600 LaSalle Road
Suite 382
Baltimore, MD 21286
(410) 296-0233
(800) ABCD-123

For information about Down syndrome and the mentally retarded:

American Association on Mental
Deficiency
(800) 424-3688

American Association on Mental
Retardation
1719 Kalorama Road, NW
Washington, DC 20009
(202) 387-1968

Association for the Help of Retarded
Children
200 Park Avenue South
New York, NY 10003
(212) 254-8203

The Association for Retarded Citizens
of the United States (ARC)
500 East Border Street
Suite 300
Arlington, TX 76010
(817) 261-6003
(800) 433-5255
(800) 232-4773

National Down Syndrome Society
666 Broadway
New York, NY 10012
(800) 221-4602

President's Committee on Mental
Retardation
U.S. Department of Health and
Human Services
Room 5325, Wilbur J. Cohen Building
330 Independence Avenue
Washington, DC 20201
(202) 619-0634

For information about rare disorders:

National Organization for Rare
Disorders (NORD)
P.O. Box 8923
New Fairfield, CT 06812-1783
(203) 746-6518
(800) 999-NORD

For information about stuttering:

Foundation for Fluency
2100 North Elston Avenue
Chicago, IL 60614
(312) 252-8800
(708) 677-5452

National Council on Stuttering
9242 Gross Point Road, #305
Skokie, IL 60077
(708) 677-5452
(708) 677-8282

National Stuttering Project
2151 Irving Street, Suite 208
San Francisco, CA 94122-1020
(415) 566-5324
(800) 364-1677

Stuttering Foundation of America
123 Oxford Road
New Rochelle, NY 10804
(914) 632-3925

For information about recovery from traumatic brain injury:

National Head Injury Foundation
1776 Massachusetts Avenue, NW
Suite 100
Washington, DC 20036
(202) 296-6443
(800) 444-NHIF

National Rehabilitation Information
    Center
8455 Colesville Road
Suite 935
Silver Spring, MD 20910
(301) 588-9284
(800) 34-NARIC
in Florida (800) 433-7022

For information about voice disorders:

Voice Foundation
1721 Pine Street
Philadephia, PA 19103
(215) 735-7999

Appendix B

Suggested Reading

On speech development:

Brooks, Mary. (1978). *Your Child's Speech and Language: Guidelines for Parents.* Austin, TX: Pro-Ed.

Parent Articles. Tucson, AZ: Communication Skill Builders.

Schwartz, Sue, and Heller, Joan. (1988). *The Language of Toys: Teaching Communication Skills to Special Needs Children.* Rockville, MD: Woodbine House.

Of general interest to parents of children with disabilities:

Armstrong, Thomas. (1987). *In Their Own Way: Discovering and Encouraging Your Child's Personal Learning Style.* Los Angeles, CA: Jeremy Tarcher, Inc.

Batshaw, Mark L., and Perret, Yvonne M. (1986). *Children with Handicaps: A Medical Primer.* Baltimore, MD: Paul H. Brookes.

Batshaw, Mark. (1991). *Your Child Has a Disability.* New York: Little/Brown.

Callanan, Charles. (1990). *Since Owen: A Parent-to-Parent Guide for the Care of a Disabled Child.* Baltmore, MD: John Hopkins.

Featherstone, Helen. (1980). *A Difference in the Family: Life with a Disabled Child.* New York, NY: Basic Books, Inc.

Lindemann, James E., and Lindemann, Sally J. (1988). *Growing Up Proud: A*

Parent's Guide to the Psychological Care of Children with Disabilities. New York, NY: Warner Books.

Moore, Cory. (1990). *A Reader's Guide for Parents of Children with Mental, Physical, or Emotional Disabilities.* Rockville, MD: Woodbine House.

Pueschel, Siegfried. (1988). *The Special Child: A Source Book for Parents of Children with Developmental Disabilities.* Baltimore, MD: Paul H. Brookes.

Simons, Robin. (1987). *After the Tears: Parents Talk about Raising a Child with a Disability.* San Diego, CA: Harcourt Brace Jovanovich.

Thompson, Charlotte E. (1986). *Raising a Handicapped Child: A Helpful Guide for Parents of the Physically Disabled.* New York, NY: William Morrow.

Tingy-Michaelis, Carol. (1983). *Handicapped Infants and Children: A Handbook for Parents and Professionals.* Baltimore, MD: University Park Press.

Weiner, Roberta, and Koppelman, Jane. (1987). *From Birth to 5: Serving the Youngest Handicapped Children.* Alexandria, VA: Capitol Publications.

On Attention Deficit Disorder:

Taylor, John F. (1990). *The Hyperactive/Attention Deficit Child.* Prima Publishing.

On cerebral palsy:

Finnie, Nancy. (1993). *Handling the Young Cerebral Palsied Child at Home.* New York, NY: Plume.

On Down syndrome and mental retardation:

Mather, June. (1981). *Make the Most of your Baby.* Arlington, TX: Association for Retarded Citizens. (Available from Association for Retarded Citizens, National Headquarters, 2501 Ave J., Arlington, TX 76006.)

Pueschel, Siegfried. (1990). *A Parent's Guide to Down Syndrome: Toward a Brighter Future.* Baltimore, MD: Paul H. Brookes.

Trainer, Marilyn. (1991). *Differences in Common: Straight Talk on Mental Retardation, Down Syndrome, and Life.* Rockville MD: Woodbine House.

On hearing impairment and related issues:

Adams, John W. (1988). *You and Your Hearing-Impaired Child.* Clerc Books.

Tye-Murray, Ed. (1992). *Cochlear Implants and Children: A Handbook for Parents, Teachers, and Speech and Hearing Professionals.* Washington, D.C: Alexander Graham Bell Association for the Deaf.

On stuttering:

Speech Foundation of America. (1989). *Stuttering and Your Child: Questions and Answers.* Memphis, TN: Speech Foundation of America.

Treiber, Patricia. (1993). *Keys to Dealing with Stuttering.* Barron's Parenting Keys.

On U.S. special education laws:

Anderson, Winifred; Chitwood, Stephen; and Hayden, Deidre. (1990). *Negotiating the Special Education Maze: A Guide for Parents and Teachers.* Rockville, MD: Woodbine House.

Glossary

age equivalent (AE): A number used on a report that indicates how a child's performance compares to normal developing children. The number is given in years and months. A child who scored an age equivalency of 9–7 on a test performed as a 9-year, 7-month-old "typical" child would have been expected to perform.

anklyoglossia: Also known as *tongue tie*. The connective tissue under the tongue (frenum) is too close to the tongue tip, resulting in restricted mobility or discomfort when talking or swallowing.

anomia: Inability to remember familiar words due to brain injury.

aphasia: Loss of previously learned language skills due to an injury of the brain.

apraxia: Difficulty making or planning movements when desired.

articulation: The way sounds are pronounced when spoken.

articulation delay: Difficulty pronouncing words clearly at the expected age.

Asberger syndrome: A mild form of autism (or related syndrome) characterized by difficulty understanding and responding to social situations.

attention deficit: Difficulty in sustaining attention.

Attention Deficit Disorder (ADD): A physical disorder characterized by distractibility, impulsiveness, and difficulty attending to one task or person for normal periods of time. The child may or may not also be hyperactive.

audiologist: The trained specialist who can determine how well a person hears and recommend educational programs or equipment to meet the needs of that person.

Audiometric Pure-Tone Threshold Test: A standard hearing test that requires the person to listen to a series of beeps at different pitches and loudness levels through headphones. When the person hears a sound, he or she raises the hand or performs some other motion.

auditory comprehension: The ability to understand what was heard.

auditory discrimination: The ability to distinguish subtle differences in similar sounds.

auditory disorders: Conditions related to the way sound or language is perceived, remembered, or comprehended.

Auditory Integration Therapy (AIT): A therapeutic program used to reduce a child's intolerance to noise and sound.

auditory memory: The ability to remember what was said.

auditory processing: The ability to take information that is heard and understand it.

auditory sequencing: The ability to hear a series of sounds or words and remember them in the same order.

auditory trainer: See **FM system.**

augmentative and alternative communication (AAC): A form of communication used by nonverbal children; often a device operated with eye blinks or by touch.

autism: A biological disorder characterized by an inability to process and use language, social, and sensory information in a normal way.

CCC-SLP: An acronym that stands for Certificate of Clinical Competency, which is awarded by the American Speech-Language-Hearing Association upon completion of a master's degree in the field, coursework in specified areas, a national exam, and a nine-month period of supervision.

central auditory processing disorder: A disorder characterized by difficulty attending to or processing speech in difficult or distracting listening environments.

cerebral palsy: A term used to describe the group of disorders that affect the way a child's muscles move.

chronological age: A person's actual age, listed in years and months on reports, such as 7–4 (7 years, 4 months old).

cleft palate: A birth defect caused by the failure of the roof of the mouth (palate) to fuse properly, resulting in an opening on the roof of the mouth that leads into the nasal cavity.

consultation time: The amount of time a specialist will meet with the classroom teacher and/or other specialists to discuss the needs and goals of a child. In the United States, this should be listed on the IEP.

deficit: A weak or below-average level of functioning in a particular skill area.

developmental apraxia: A form of apraxia considered to be maturational in nature.

developmental delay: A delay in achieving certain skills when expected. It is usually associated with infants and children under the age of 7.

disorder: A permanent condition characterized by a weakness in one or more skill areas.

divergent language skills: The ability to organize language and respond to open-ended or general questions, such as "Tell me about your trip."

Down syndrome: A genetic condition associated with mental retardation and specific physical characteristics.

dysarthric: Describes an articulation pattern that sounds slurred or labored; associated with neurological disorders or brain damage.

dysfluency: The professional term for stuttering.

echolalia: A pattern of responding to questions or comments by repeating what was heard or the last part of it. Echolalia is associated with autism.

exceptionality: A handicapping condition; term used in Canadian schools.

expressive language: Spoken or written words and sentences that express our thoughts.

expressive vocabulary: The collection of words a person uses when speaking.

facilitated communication: A technique used with autistic and physically impaired people whereby another person (known as a *facilitator*) supports the wrist or arm of the handicapped person while the person touches or types the letters on a keyboard. The letters form words that are thought by many to express the handicapped person's thoughts.

fluency: The ability to speak in a natural flow without hesitating or stuttering.

FM system: An electronic device that helps hearing-impaired or distractible children to focus on the teacher's voice. It consists of a lapel-sized microphone clipped to the teacher's collar, which is wired to a small transistor-sized box worn on a belt. The child receives the teacher's voice through a loop, headphones, or attachment to the hearing aid (if worn), which is also wired to a similar box worn on a belt.

formal tests: See **standardized tests.**

inclusion: A currently popular educational philosophy that values placing any child with a handicapping condition in a regular classroom as opposed to a segregated classroom with other handicapped children.

Individualized Educational Plan (IEP): The formal document used (and required) across the United States for children ages 3 to 15 that details the nature of a child's handicapping condition and how it will be accommodated in the school.

Individualized Family Service Plan (IFSP): An IEP for a child under the age of 3.

informal tests: Tests administered by observing the child perform specific tasks in a natural environment, such as interacting with other children, playing with puppets, or responding to conversational questions.

language-learning disability: A learning disability affecting the performance of language-related tasks. Most learning disabilities are language-learning disabilities.

larynx: The structure that houses the vocal cords.

learning disabilities consultant: A specialist who diagnoses the presence of a learning disability and recommends an appropriate program for the child with learning disabilities. Also known as a *special education teacher* or *resource room teacher.*

learning disability: A disorder characterized by a discrepancy between a child's ability (which must be measured as average or higher on an IQ test) and classroom performance that is not due to an emotional or physical handicap.

lisp: A speech problem characterized by the distortion of the *s* and *z* sounds.

listening disorders: Any condition that causes a child to have difficulty hearing or listening normally.

metalinguistics: The ability to talk about and understand language concepts, such as counting syllables and words or knowing the difference between a letter and a word.

MLU: Acronym for "mean length of utterance." An index of language development based on the number of words per sentence that is used to assess language quantity.

modification: A term used on the IEP that details what changes will be made in the classroom to accommodate a child's handicapping condition.

morphological deficit: Difficulty in using the correct endings (such as the *ed* in walk*ed*) or tenses (*ran* as opposed to *runned*) of words.

morphology: The sounds or syllables on the beginning or end of a word that affect its meaning. For example, the *s* on the word *cars* shows there is more than one car; the plural *s* gives us information about the car.

nodules: See **vocal nodules.**

obturator: An appliance worn in the mouth by a child with a cleft palate that allows more normal eating and speaking.

occupational therapist: A professional who evaluates and facilitates the development of fine motor skills.

oral-apraxia: The inability to plan or carry out movements with precision or ease when using the muscles in the mouth area.

oral-motor skills: The ability to perform certain functions and movements with the tongue, lips, cheeks, and other muscles of the mouth area.

oral-motor weakness: Difficulty moving or controlling the muscles in the mouth area needed for chewing, swallowing, and speaking.

otitis media: A middle ear infection, usually accompanied by the presence of fluid behind the eardrum.

otolaryngologist: An ear, nose and throat doctor.

papilloma: A growth, similar to a wart, viral in nature, which can cause hoarseness and, if left untreated, grow and multiply, obstructing the airway.

percentile rank: See **percentiles.**

percentiles: A number that compares a person's performance on a test to others of the same age. A person receiving a percentile of 25 scored better than 25 percent of people the same age who took the test in a massive sampling before the test was published.

Pervasive Developmental Delay (PDD): A term used to describe infants and toddlers who display delays in acquiring skills in most or all areas.

phonological disorder: A disorder characterized by difficulty understanding the rules used for combining sounds to pronounce words, resulting in significant speech errors.

phonology: The aspect of language dealing with the production and understanding of sounds.

pragmatics: How language is used in social situations.

receptive language: Language that is understood and comprehended. This can be heard, read, or interpreted from body language.

receptive vocabulary: The words a person is able to understand.

referential skills: The ability to make others understand what is being talked about. For example, if a child says "Mom, he isn't nice" after coming home from school, the child is not using good referential skills. You don't know whom the child is referring to because it is out of context.

semantics: The way words are used to convey the intended meaning.

sensory integration deficits: Difficulties with interpreting information the body takes in from the sensory organs, such as hearing, seeing, and touch. Generally found in preschool and young elementary school children as well as autistic children.

sequencing: Putting things in the correct order.

speech clinician: See **speech-language pathologist.**

speech discrimination: The ability to distinguish similar sounding words.

speech-language pathologist (SLP): The specialist who diagnoses and provides treatment for speech, language, and listening disorders.

speech pathologist: See **speech-language pathologist.**

speech therapist: See **speech-language pathologist.**

standard deviation (SD): The amount of difference between the performance of an average child and another child. A standard deviation of −2.0 or more signifies a deficit on a particular skill tested.

standardized tests: Tests commercially prepared, containing statistical information about the performance expectations of a "normal" child on each subtest. It usually provides percentiles and age equivalents, among other statistics, for comparison.

stanines: A way of comparing a child's performance, based on a 1 to 9 designation, with 5 being average.

syntax: The order of words that combine to form a grammatical sentence.

syntax deficit: Problems with organizing and using words in the proper order to form a grammatical sentence.

tongue thrust: An imbalance of the tongue muscles observable when swallowing or at rest, frequently causing mild articulation errors and/ or dental problems. The tongue pushes forward between the teeth instead of moving backward when swallowing.

traumatic brain injury (TBI): Any sudden damage to the brain after birth.

tympanogram: The graph that shows the results of a test performed with a tympanometer.

tympanometer: An instrument that measures or detects the presence of fluid or abnormal pressure in the ear.

vocabulary: Words.

vocal abuse: A pattern of speaking or using the voice that causes hoarseness and irritation of the vocal cords.

vocal nodules: Small growths that grow on the vocal cords as a result of ongoing irritation, resulting in hoarseness and difficulty using the voice.

vocal polyps: Fluid-filled sacs that can form on the lining of the vocal cords.

word-finding problems: See **word retrieval deficit.**

word retrieval deficit: Difficulty in thinking of a familiar word on the spot.

Bibliography

Aderson, Winifred; Chitwood, Stephen; and Hayden, Deidre. (1990). *Negotiating the Special Education Maze: A Guide for Parents and Teachers*. Rockville, MD: Woodbine House.

Bicklen, Douglas. (1992). Typing to talk: Facilitated communication. *American Journal of Speech-Language Pathology, 1*(1), 15–27.

Blosser, Jean L., and DePompei, Roberta. (1989). The head-injured student returns to school: Recognizing and treating deficits. *Topics in Language Disorders, 9*(2), 67–78.

Boone, Daniel R. (1983). *The Voice and Voice Therapy,* 3rd ed. Englewood Cliffs, NJ: Prentice-Hall.

Brooks, Mary. (1978). *Your Child's Speech and Language: Guidelines for Parents.* Austin, TX: Pro-Ed.

Conture, Edward, ed. (1989). *Stuttering and Your Child: Questions and Answers.* Memphis, TN: Speech Foundation of America.

Costello, Janis, and Holland, Audrey. (1986). *Handbook of Speech and Language Disorders*. San Diego, CA: College-Hill Press.

Department of Education, State of Connecticut. (1993). *Guidelines for Speech and Language Programs.*

Fowler, Mary. (1992). *C.H.A.D.D. Educators Manual: An In-Depth Look at Attention Deficit Disorders from an Educational Perspective.* Plantation, FL: C.H.A.D.D.

Friel-Patti, Sandy, and Finitzo, Terese. (1990). Language learning in a prospective study of otitis media with effusion in the first two years of life. *Journal of Speech and Hearing Research, 33,* 188–194.

Garrard, Kay Russell, and Clark, Bertha Smith. (1985). Otitis media: The role of the speech and language pathologists. *ASHA, 27*(7), 35–39.

Gerber, Adele, and Bryen, Diane N. (1981). *Guide to Language and Learning Disabilities.* Phoenix, AZ: ECL Publications.

Giddan, Jane J. (1991). School-children with emotional problems and communication deficits: Implications for speech-language pathologists. *Language, Speech, and Hearing Services in Schools, 1,* 291–295.

Goldberger, Jeanne M. (1978). *Tongue Thrust Correction.* Danville, IL: Interstate Printers & Publishers, Inc.

Gordon, Pearl A., and Luper, Harold L. (1992). The early identification of beginning stuttering II: Problems. *American Journal of Speech-Language Pathology: A Journal of Clinical Practice, 1,* 49–55.

Gravel, Judith S., and Wallace, Ina F. (1992). Listening and language at 4 years of age: Effect of early otitis media. *Journal of Speech and Hearing Research, 35,* 588–595.

Hall, Joseph W., and Grose, John H. (1993). The effect of otitis media with effusion on the masking-level difference and the auditory brainstem response. *Journal of Speech and Hearing Research, 36,* 210–217.

Hasenstab, M. Suzanne. (1987). *Language Learning and Otitis Media.* Boston, MA: College-Hill.

Jansky, J., and de Hirsch, K. (1973). *Preventing Reading Failure.* New York: Harper & Row.

Keith, Robert W. (1981). *Auditory and Language Disorders in Children.* San Diego, CA: College Hill Press, Inc.

Kidd, K. K. (1977). A genetic perspective on stuttering. *Journal of Fluency Disorders, 2,* 259–269.

Lewis, Barbara, and Freebairn, Lisa. (1992). Residual effects of preschool phonology disorders in grade school, adolescence, and adulthood. *Journal of Speech and Hearing Research, 35,* 819–831.

Mack, Alison E., and Warr-Leeper, Genese A. (1992). Language abilities in boys with chronic behavior disorders. *Language, Speech, and Hearing Services in Schools, 23,* 214–223.

Myer, Charles M. III. (1992). Fluctuating hearing loss in children. *American Journal of Audiology: A Journal of Clinical Practice, 1,* 25–26.

Onslow, Mark. (1992). Identification of early stuttering: Issues and suggested strategies. *American Journal of Speech-Language Pathology: A Journal of Clinical Practice, 1,* 21–27.

Onslow, Mark; Costa, Leanne; and Rue, Stephen. (1990). Direct early intervention with stuttering: Some preliminary data. *Journal of Speech and Hearing Disorders, 55,* 405–416.

Owens, Robert E., Jr. (1988). *Language Development.* Columbus, OH: Merrill Publishing Co.

Oyer, Herbert J.; Crowe, Barbara; Haas, William H. (1987). *Speech, Language, & Hearing Disorders: A Guide for the Teacher.* Needham, MA: Allyn and Bacon.

Prizant, Barry; Audet, Lisa R.; Burke, Grace M.; Hummel, Lauren J.; Maher, Suzanne R.; and Theadore, Geraldine. (1990). Communication disorders and emotional/behavioral disorders in children and adolescents. *Journal of Speech and Hearing Disorders, 55,* 179–192.

Pueschel, Siegfried. (1990). *A Parent's Guide to Down Syndrome.* Baltimore, MD: Paul H. Brookes.

Rice, Mabel L.; Sell, Marie A.; Hadley, Pamela A. (1991). Social interactions of speech-and-language-impaired children. *Journal of Speech and Hearing Research, 34,* 1299–1307.

Roberts, Joanne E.; Burchinal, Margaret R.; Davis, Brenda P.; Collier, Albert M.; and Henderson, Frederick W. (1991). Otitis media in early childhood and later language. *Journal of Speech and Hearing Research, 34,* 1158–1168.

Seifert, Holly, and Schwartz, Ilsa. (1991). Treatment effectiveness of large group basic concept instruction with Head Start students. *Language, Speech and Hearing Services in Schools, 22,* 60–64.

Sloan, Christine. (1986). *Treating Auditory Processing Difficulties in Children.* Boston, MA: College-Hill Press.

Smoski, Walter J.; Brunt, Michael A.; and Tannahill, Curtis. (1992). Listening characteristics of children with central auditory processing disorders. *Language, Speech, and Hearing Services in Schools, 23,* 145–152.

Snyder, Lynn S., and Downey, Doris M. (1991). The language-reading relationship in normal and reading-disabled children. *Journal of Speech and Hearing Research, 34,* 129–140.

Snyder-McLean, L., and McLean, J. (1987). Effectiveness of early intervention for children with language and communication disorders. In M. Guaralnick and J. Bennett (Eds.), *The Effectiveness of Early Intervention for At-Risk and Handicapped Children,* 213–274. Orlando, FL: Academic Press.

Stedman, Donald J. (1989–1990). The essential value of early education. *National Student Speech Language Hearing Association Journal, 17,* 29–38.

Swank, Linda K., and Catts, Hugh W. (1994). Phonological awareness and written word decoding. *Language, Speech, and Hearing Services in Schools, 25,* 9–14.

Tallal, Paula. (1976). Rapid auditory processing in normal and disordered language development. *Journal of Speech and Hearing Research, 19,* 561–571.

Tomblin, J. Bruce; Hardy, James C.; and Hein, Herman A. (1991). Predicting poor communication status in preschool children using risk factors present at birth. *Journal of Speech and Hearing Research, 34,* 1096–1105.

Trace, Robert. (1992). Early intervention is the key. *Advance,* May 4, 1992.

Van Riper, Charles. (1978). *Speech Correction: Principles and Methods.* Englewood Cliffs, NJ: Prentice-Hall.

Wallach, Geraldine, P., and Miller, Lynda. (1988). *Language Intervention and Academic Success.* Boston, MA: College-Hill Press.

Warren, S., and Kaiser, A. (1988). Research in early language intervention. In S. Odom and M. Karnes (Eds.), *Early Intervention for Infants and Children with Handicaps: An Empirical Base,* 89–108. Baltimore, MD: Paul H. Brookes.

Whitehurst, Grover J.; Arnold, David S.; Smith, Meagan; Fischel, Janet E.; Lonigan, Christopher J.; and Valdez-Menchaca, Marta C. (1991). Family history in developmental expressive language delay. *Journal of Speech and Hearing Research, 34,* 1150–1157.

Wilcox, Jeanne M., and Caswell, Susan B. (1991). Early language intervention: A comparison of classroom and individual treatment. *American Journal of Speech-Language Pathology, 1,* 49–62.

Index